DRUG I.D. & SYMPTOM GUIDE

6th Edition

QWIK-CODES™

Printed in the United States of America.

QWIK-CODES is a trademark of QWIK-CODES.

Published by
QWIK-CODES

sales@qwik-codes.com

Comments & suggestions are welcome.

Typesetting and production by The McNaughton Group
www.mcnaughtongroup.com

v.11.06.14

ISBN: 978-1-56325-224-2

EISBN: 978-1-56325-225-9

EDITORIAL CONTRIBUTIONS & SPECIAL THANKS

EDITED BY

Sgt. Keith Graves has been a police officer in California since 1990. He is a Drug Recognition Expert Instructor (IACP #3292) and teaches both the DRE course and the CNOA Drug Abuse Recognition Course. Keith has also taught at the Basic Police Academy and has developed a number of POST certified drug courses. Among other assignments, Keith has served as a Narcotics/Vice Detective. To request a tailored training course for your department, or to attend an existing course, visit www.gravesassociates.com.

For up-to-date Street Drug information, visit: www.gravesassociates.com

SPECIAL THANKS TO

Trinka Porrata, Contributing Editor, President, Project GHB. www.projectghb.org

Gil VanAttenhoven, Training Director, California Narcotic Officers' Association. www.cnoa.org

Teri Bennett, Supervising Investigator, Medical Board of California, for her photo contributions of Butalbital, Demerol vials, Provigil, OxyContin and Zyprexa.

CONTENTS

CONTENTS

CANNABIS

MARIJUANA

Cannabis

Dried Marijuana

Marijuana Leaf

MARIJUANA

Cannabis

Visual Description

A dried, green leafy substance mixed with stems and possibly seeds.

Methods of Use

Ingested, Smoked

Effects

Onset: 8–10 Seconds
Peak: 10–30 Minutes
Duration: 6–8 Hours

Primary Symptoms of Use

Nystagmus: No
Lack of Convergence: Yes
Pulse: Elevated
Pupils: Normal to Dilated
Pupillary Reaction to Light: Normal
Blood Pressure: Elevated
Body Temperature: Near normal

Other Symptoms

Bloodshot eyes
Body tremors
Debris in mouth
Difficulty concentrating
Disoriented
Eyelid tremors
Impaired divided attention
Impaired time/distance perception
Increased appetite
Odor of burning marijuana
Pupillary unrest
Relaxed inhibitions

Overdose Symptoms

Fatigue
Paranoia
Psychosis

Additional Comments

Commercially made packets labeled with names like Spice, Gold Spice, Yucatan Fire, etc. were shown to contain a variety of herbs plus verifiable amounts of synthetic cannabinoids or cannabinoid-mimicking compounds, including HU-210 and/or JWH-018. These compounds are commonly called "Spice" and are synthetic cannabinoids that are more potent than THC. As states pass laws to outlaw "Spice", manufacturers change their formulation so they can skirt the law. There are now over 200 formulations. For more information, see **Synthetic Cannabinoids** on page 14.

MARIJUANA CIGARETTE

Thai Sticks

Packaged Marijuana and Marijuana Cigarettes

MARIJUANA CIGARETTE

Slang Terms

Blunt
Joint
Fatty
Dooby
Reefer

Visual Description

A dried, green leafy substance mixed with stems and possibly seeds, hand-rolled into a cigarette (joint).

Methods of Use

Smoked

Duration of Effects

Onset: 8–10 Seconds
Peak: 10–30 Minutes
Duration: Variable

Primary Symptoms of Use

Nystagmus: No
Pupils: Normal (possibly dilated)
Pulse: Elevated
Blood Pressure: Elevated
Body Temperature: Near normal
Lack of Convergence: Yes

Other Symptoms

Bloodshot eyes
Body tremors
Debris in mouth
Difficulty concentrating
Disoriented
Eyelid tremors
Impaired divided attention
Impaired time/distance perception
Increased appetite
Odor of burning marijuana
Pupillary unrest
Relaxed inhibitions

Overdose Symptoms

Fatigue
Paranoia
Psychosis

MARIJUANA GROW

Marijuana "Grow"

Marijuana "Grow" showing individual potted plants.

MARIJUANA GROW

To establish evidence for a cultivation charge

- Photographically document the roots of plants to demonstrate live plant status at time of seizure.
- Document/seize evidence such as weighing devices and articles showing identity of persons in control of premises.
- Outdoor cultivation—pipes (buried or above ground), hoses or other evidence of irrigation systems consistent with marijuana cultivation; other trees, shrubs or plants planted or maintained to hide marijuana plants from view; gardening tools, fertilizer, seeds, sheds/facilities for hanging, drying, processing and packaging for distribution; security devices or systems such as video surveillance, booby traps and armed security personnel.
- Indoor cultivation—grow lights, tubing or hoses or pipes arranged for use as an irrigation system for watering individual plants or maintaining a hydroponic garden; seeds, plant medium, various sizes of pots, foil to cover walls and/or ceilings to reflect light and heat inward (improving growth patterns and/or limiting heat escape); transformers, heating/cooling and lighting systems for cultivation; security systems; facilities for hanging, drying, processing, storing, packaging and mailing of marijuana.
- Also: literature, magazines and computer data regarding cultivation techniques, especially those specific to marijuana; pays and owes regarding distribution of narcotics.
- Computer equipment or electronic storage devices, handwritten notes or printed confidential password lists to enter secured files; indicators of Internet usage and "favorite" or "bookmarked" Internet locations dealing with the use, cultivation and trafficking of marijuana and other narcotics.

HASHISH OIL

Butane Hash Oil

Butane Hash Oil

HASHISH OIL

Slang terms

Dabs
BHO
Wax
Earwax

Butane Hash Oil

The latest form of hash oil to appear on the market is Butane Hash Oil (BHO). BHO is simple to make. Manufacturers of BHO will place marijuana into a cylinder, usually made of glass, stainless steel, or PVC pipe. End caps will be placed on both ends. Butane will be injected into the cylinder on the top end. The butane will cover the marijuana inside of the cylinder and then drain out of the bottom of the cylinder and into a Pyrex dish. This process removes THC from the plant material inside of the cylinder. THC purity rates can reach up to 90% with this method. However, the explosive potential is very real. A number of deaths have occurred as a result of this process.

Visual Description

Concentrated, thick liquid, dark or gold in color.

Methods of Use

Smoked in a blunt or in a special bong. Can also be smoked off the tip of a nail, paper clip, or similar object.

Effects

Onset: 8–10 Seconds
Peak: 10–30 Minutes
Duration: 4–6 Hours (variable)

Primary Symptoms of Use

Nystagmus: No
Lack of Convergence: Yes
Pulse: Elevated
Pupils: Normal to Dilated
Pupillary Reaction to Light: Normal
Blood Pressure: Elevated
Body Temperature: Near Normal

Other Symptoms

Bloodshot eyes
Body tremors
Debris in mouth
Difficulty concentrating
Disoriented
Eyelid tremors
Impaired divided attention
Impaired time/distance perception
Increased appetite
Odor of burning marijuana
Pupillary unrest
Relaxed inhibitions

Overdose Symptoms

Fatigue
Paranoia
Psychosis

HASHISH

Hashish in bag used for transportation.

Hashish and bag shown with 10 cent coin for comparison.

Kief: Made by placing marijuana leaves in a silk screen and gently shaking. The dust that settles is pictured above and goes by the name Kief. It is considered concentrated cannabis (hashish).

HASHISH

Visual Description

Solid dark green, brownish, or gold substance. Can be a solid or powder form.

Methods of Use

Ingested, Smoked

Effects

Onset: 8–10 Seconds
Peak: 10–30 Minutes
Duration: 4–6 Hours (variable)

Primary Symptoms of Use

Nystagmus: No
Lack of Convergence: Yes
Pulse: Elevated
Pupils: Normal to Dilated
Pupillary Reaction to Light: Normal
Blood Pressure: Elevated
Body Temperature: Near Normal

Other Symptoms

Bloodshot eyes
Body tremors
Debris in mouth
Difficulty concentrating
Disoriented
Eyelid tremors
Impaired divided attention
Impaired time/distance perception
Increased appetite
Odor of burning marijuana
Pupillary unrest
Relaxed inhibitions

Overdose Symptoms

Fatigue
Paranoia
Psychosis

MARIJUANA EDIBLES

These are various food products that include ground or chopped marijuana, or are infused with THC. They do cause intoxication and are considered concentrated cannabis. These products are causing ER trips for overdoses as it is difficult to control dosage and people may unknowingly ingest excessive amounts.

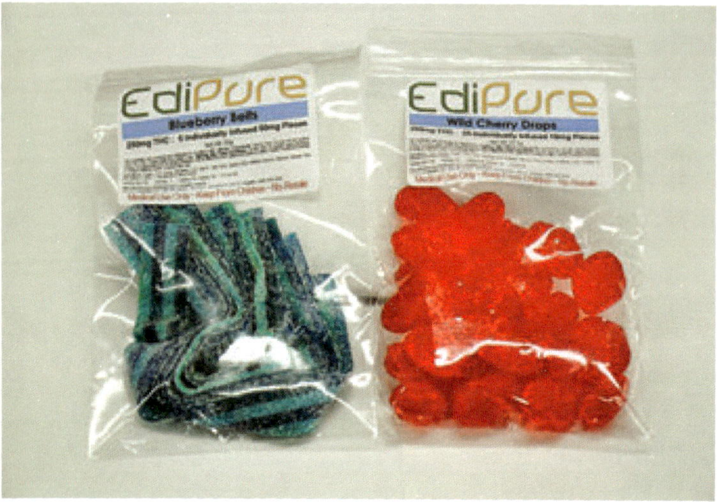

THC-Infused Candies

THC-Infused Beef Jerky and Popcorn

This page intentionally left blank.

SYNTHETIC CANNABINOIDS
(AKA: Spice or K2)

Synthetic Cannabinoid - "Spice"

(Photo courtesy of, Cpl. Susan Barge - Florida Highway Patrol)

Synthetic Cannabinoid - "Spice"

(Photo courtesy of, Cpl. Susan Barge - Florida Highway Patrol)

SYNTHETIC CANNABINOIDS
(AKA: Spice or K2)

Visual Description:

Mixture of dried herbs sprayed with synthetic cannabinoid-like substance

Methods of Use

Smoked

Effects

Effects start in less than 10 seconds
Lasts 3–5 hours depending on the potency and the amount smoked

Primary Symptoms of Use

Nystagmus: Has been present in some cases
Lack of Convergence: Yes
Pulse: Elevated
Pupils: Dilated
Pupillary Reaction to Light: Normal
Blood Pressure: Elevated
Body Temperature: Near Normal

Other Symptoms

Panic attacks,
Red conjunctiva
Tachycardia
Dry mouth
Vomiting
Hallucinations
Delusions
Increased agitation
Dilated pupils
Body temperature changes

Additional Comments

Commonly referred to as "Spice" or "K2", synthetic cannabinoids are made in China and Korea and shipped to the US. It is often sold in liquor stores, smoke shops and adult book stores. It has been described by some users as several hundred times more potent than THC, the main psychoactive compound in marijuana. Express Diagnostics International has a urine test that can detect spice.

This page intentionally left blank.

DEPRESSANTS

ALCOHOL (ETHANOL)

Visual Description

Liquid, various odors, colors & flavors. Also found in some perfumes, after-shaves, food flavorings (e.g. vanilla, almond, lemon extracts).

Effects

Onset: Rapid (varies with quantity consumed and rate of consumption)
Duration: Roughly .02 BAC metabolized per hour.

Method of Use

Ingested. Some reports of alcohol enemas in college scene. An alcohol inhalation machine (called AWOL for "alcohol without liquid") mixes alcohol with oxygen which is then inhaled. The AWOL concept has gained popularity in Asia and Europe but is meeting resistance in the U.S. and has been banned in some areas.

Symptoms

Nystagmus: Yes
Pupils: Near normal size, reaction slowed
Pulse: Elevated
Blood Pressure: Elevated
Body Temperature: Subnormal
Lack of Convergence: Yes

Other Symptoms

Euphoria
Lack of coordination
Slurred speech
Exaggerated emotional state
Reduced visual acuity, peripheral vision & glare recovery
Ataxia
Impaired judgment & reflexes
Increased pain threshold
Reduced inhibitions
Boisterous or aggressive behavior

Overdose Symptoms

Incontinence
Inability to stand or walk
Coma
Respiratory depression
Pulmonary aspiration
Death

ALCOHOL (ETHANOL)

Delirium Tremens (DT's)

May begin within 48–72 hours for chronic heavy abusers who stop their consumption of alcohol.

Additional Comments

The average adult can metabolize about 7–10 g of alcohol per hour (rate variable per individual and overall blood alcohol level). While tolerance may vary greatly in individuals, generally speaking an ethanol level below 300 mg/dL in a comatose patient presented to the ER will initiate a search for alternative causes (medical condition or other drugs).

Body Fluids Required For Testing

While breath and blood are the preferred samples for alcohol alone, urine should be considered if other drugs are suspected.

BARBITURATES

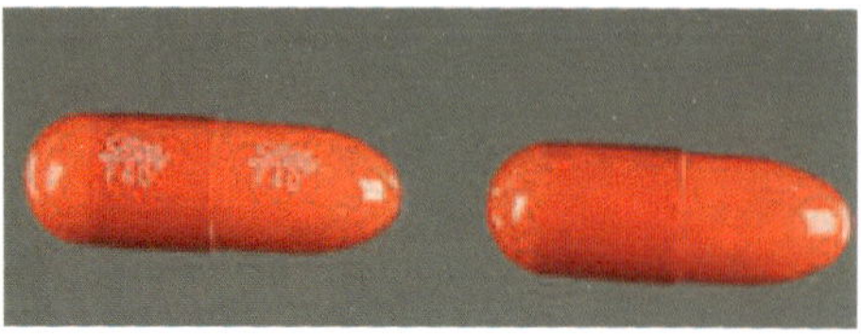

Seconal (secobarbital) Capsules

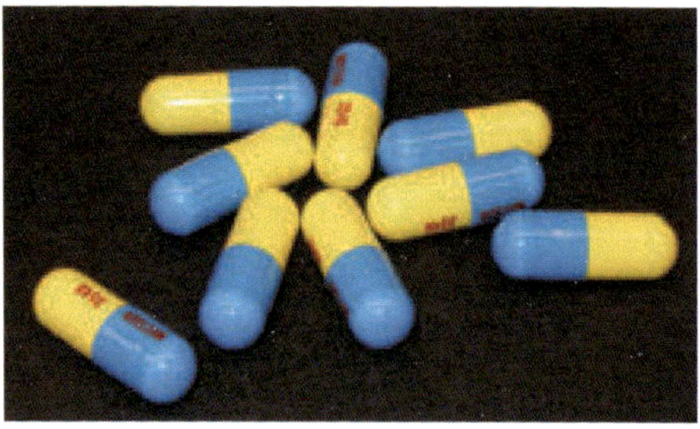

Butalbital Capsules

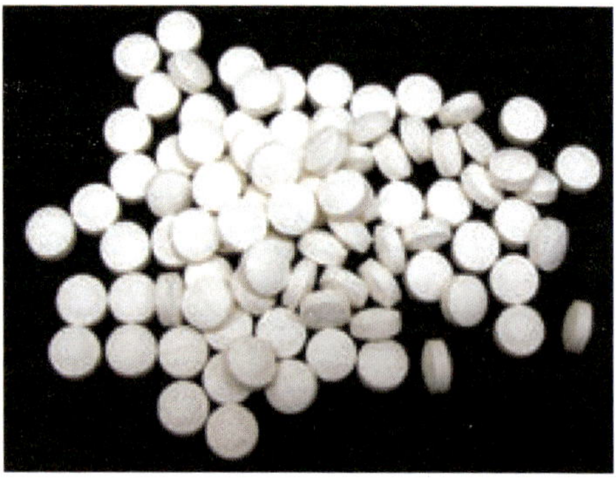

Phenobarbital Tablets

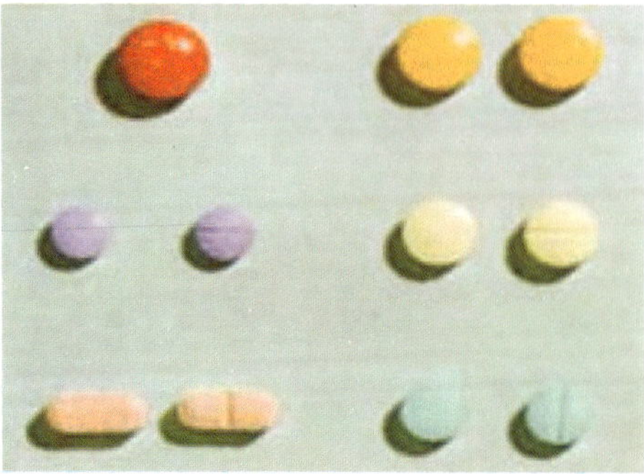

Miscellaneous Barbiturate Tablets

BARBITURATES

Drug Name—Trade Name (representative)

Amobarbital—Amytal
Butalbital—Fiorinal or Fioricet
Mephobarbital—Mebaral
Pentobarbital—Numbutal
Phenobarbital—Luminal
Secobarbital—Seconal, Tuinal
Butabarbital Sodium—Butisol
Methohexital—Brevital
Thiopental—Pentothal

Visual Description

Various colored capsules. Most commonly abused are secobarbital (red devils), pentobarbital (yellow jackets) and amobarbital (blue angels).

Methods of Use

Ingested, injected, snorted

Duration of Effects

1–16 hours depending on which drug taken.

Primary Symptoms of Use

Nystagmus: Yes

Other Symptoms

Sedation, hypnosis and/or deep coma
Anesthesia
Lethargy
Slurred speech
Ataxia
Mild to severe intoxication

Additional Comments

Barbiturates range from ultra short acting, such as methohexital and thiopental; to short acting, such as pentobarbital; to intermediate acting, such as amobarbital or butabarbital; to long acting, such as phenobarbital or methobarbital. Typically used as hypnotic/sedative agents, for induction of anesthesia, treatment of epilepsy, and as anticonvulsants.

Special Testing Notes

Short/intermediate acting barbiturates may be detected in urine 24–72 hours; longer acting barbiturates up to seven days.

NON-BARBITURATES

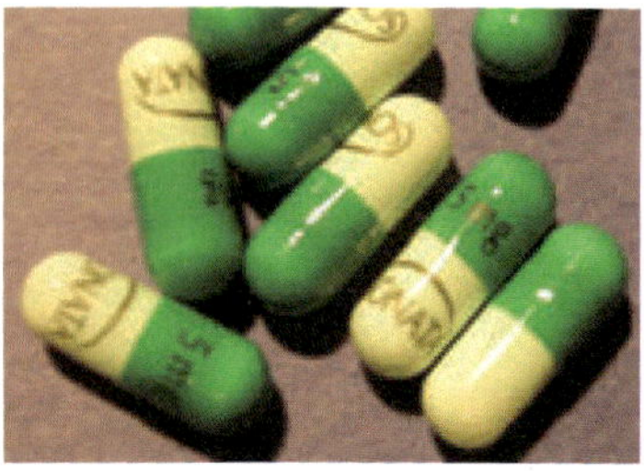

Sonata

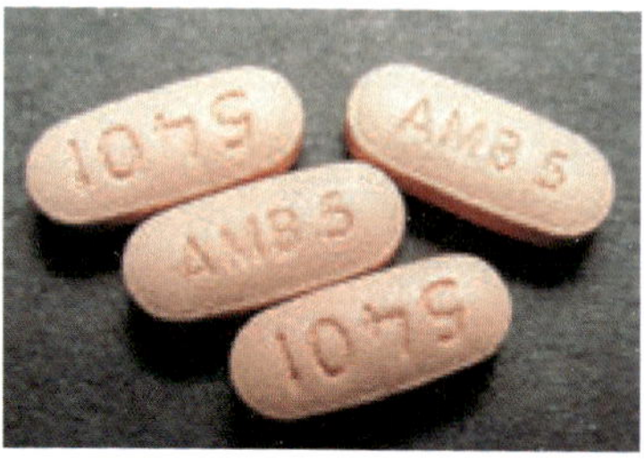

Ambien 5mg

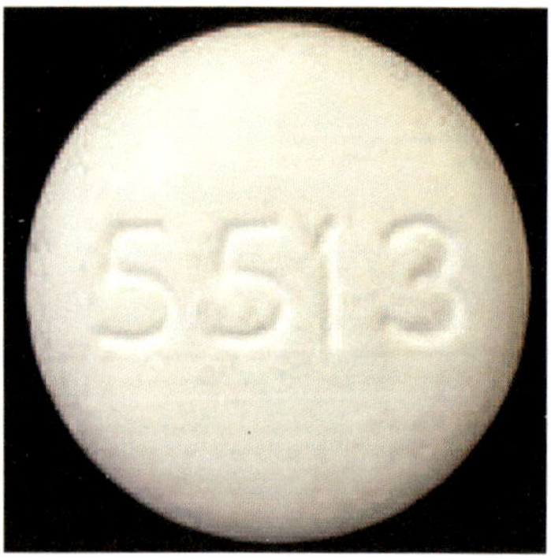

Soma [front]

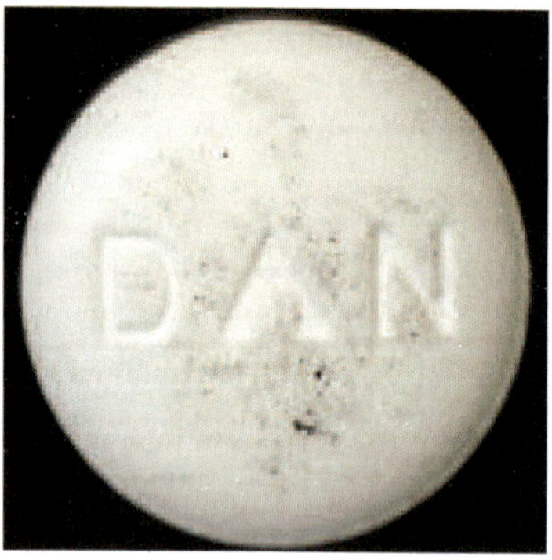

Soma [back]

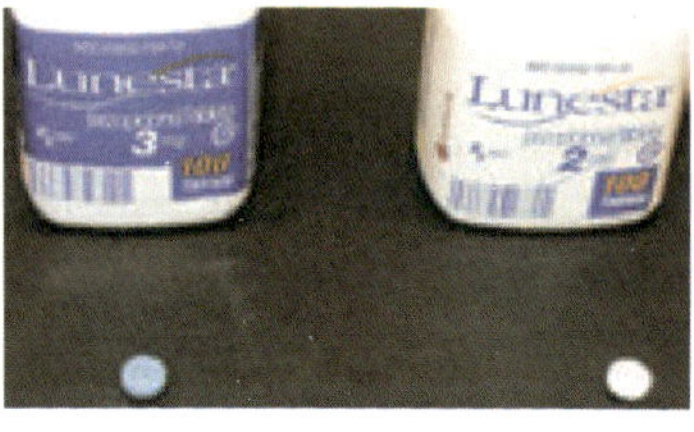

Lunesta 3mg (right) and 2mg (left)

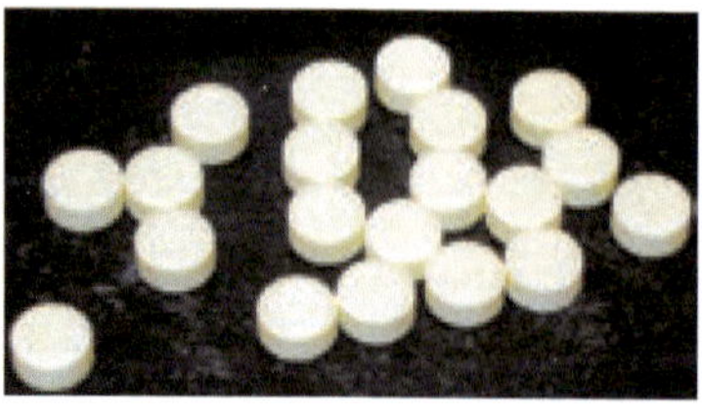

Buspirone 7.5

NON-BARBITURATES

Drug Name—Trade Name (representative)

Buspirone—BuSpar
Carisoprodol—Soma
Chloral hydrate—Noctec, Somnote, Aquachloral, Supprettes
Diphenhydramine HCl—Benadryl
Eszopiclone—Lunesta
Ethchlorvynol—Placidyl
Ethinamate – (no U.S. or Canada brand)
Glutethimide—Doriden
Meprobamate—Miltown, Equanil
Methaqualone—Quaalude
Methocarbamol—Robaxin
Methyprylon—Moludar
Paraldehyde—Paral
Zaleplon—Sonata
Zolpidem—Ambien

Visual Description

Various colors and brands of tablets.

Methods of Use

Ingested, injected, snorted

Duration of Effects

1–16 hours depending on which drug taken.

Primary Symptoms of Use

Nystagmus: Yes

Other Symptoms

Sedation, hypnosis and/or deep coma
Anesthesia
Lethargy
Slurred speech
Ataxia
Mild to severe intoxication

Additional Comments

Methaqualone pharmaceutical products were discontinued in 1984 in U.S. May see counterfeit, foreign or old stock.

While diphenhydramine is a common over the counter ingredient, it is impairing for purposes of driving and for use in drugging for robbery or rapes, etc.

Ambien has been identified in a number of drug rape cases and has been associated with "sleep driving" incidents of DUI and other sleep walking incidents in which the person has no recall of the conduct. Some people use Ambien to get high. Some users are reporting that they are experiencing hallucinations on Ambien.

ANTI-PSYCHOTIC TRANQUILIZERS

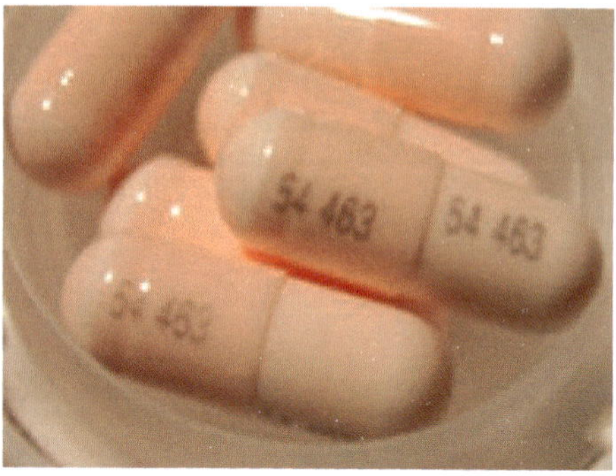

Lithium (Eskalith)

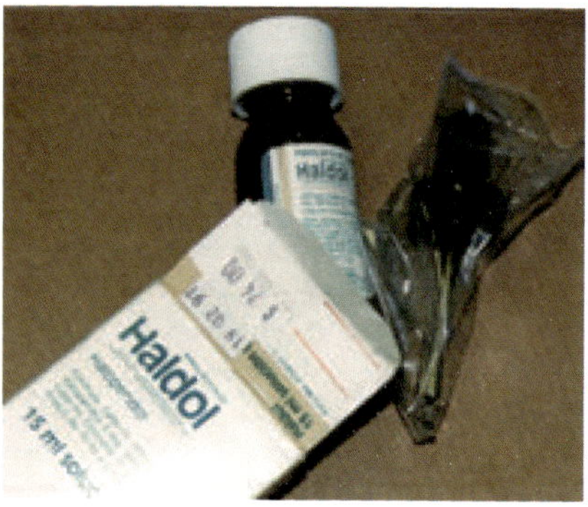

Halperidol (Haldol)

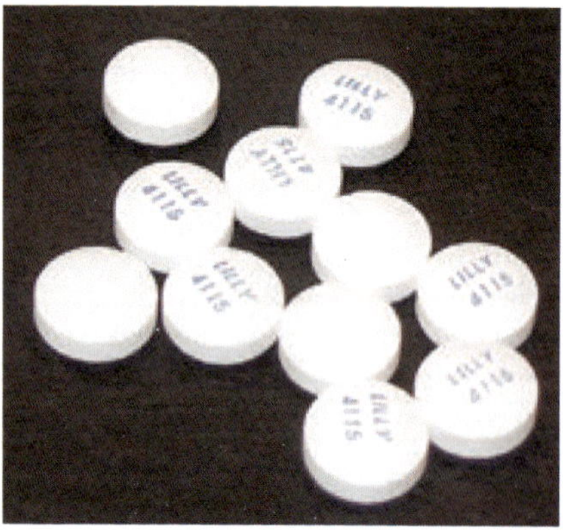

Olenzapine (Zyprexa)

ANTI-PSYCHOTIC TRANQUILIZERS

Drug Name—Trade Name (representative)

Chlorpromazine—Thorazine
Clozapine—Clozaril
Droperidol—Inapsine
Fluphenazine HCl—Prolixin
Haloperidol—Haldol
Lithium—Eskalith, Lithobid, Lithane (Canada)
Loxapine—Loxitane
Mesoridazine—Serentil
Molindone—Moban
Olanzapine—Zyprexa
Perphenazine—Trilafon
Prochlorperazine—Compazine
Promethazine—Phenergan
Risperidone—Risperdal
Seroquel—Quetiapine Fumarate
Thioridazine—Mellaril
Trimethobenzamide—Tigan

Visual Description

Various Tablets

Methods of Use

Ingested, Snorted

Primary Symptoms of Use

Mild to severe intoxication, sedation, dry mouth (Exception: Clozapine can cause hypersalivation)
Absence of sweating
Tachycardia
Coma
Seizures
Jaw muscle spasm
Respiratory arrest
Either hypothermia or hyperthermia may be seen.
Overdose may be seen in suicide attempts though some are not extremely toxic.

ANTI-ANXIETY TRANQUILIZERS

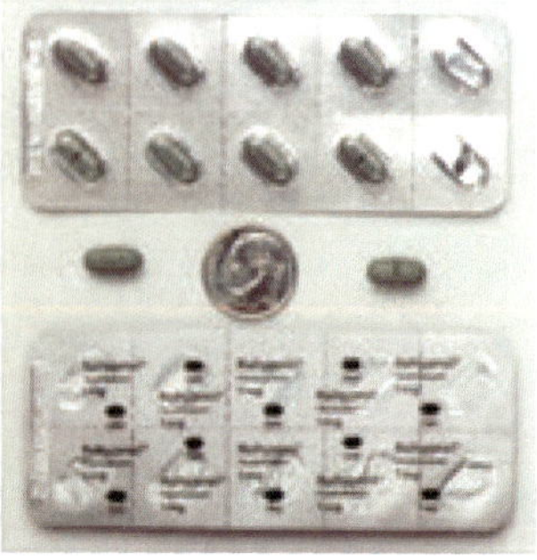

Flunitrazepam (Rohypnol)

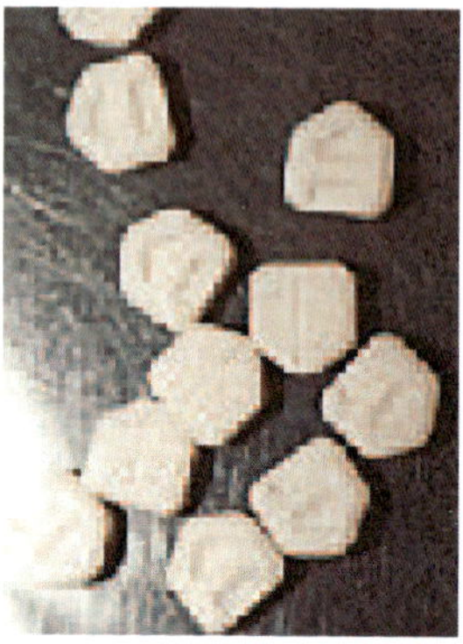

Lorazepam (Ativan)

Diazepam (Valium)

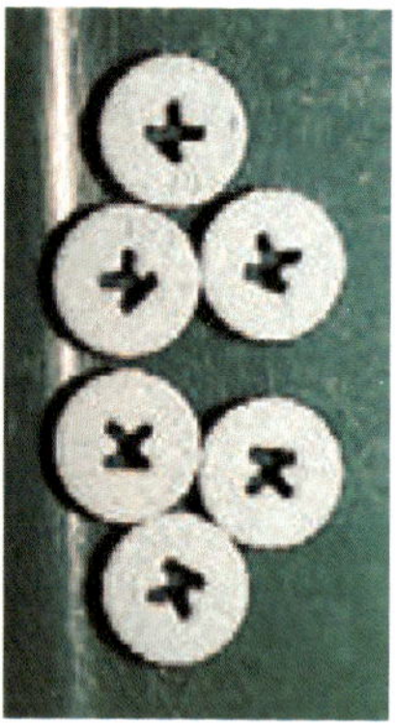

Clonazepam (Klonopin or Rivotril [Mexico])

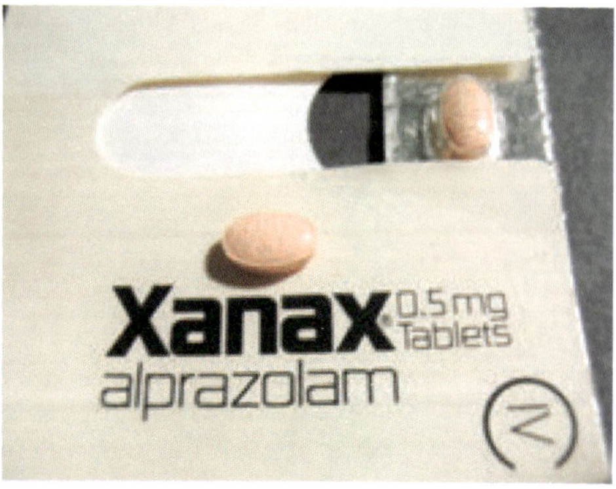

Alprazolam (Xanax)

ANTI-ANXIETY TRANQUILIZERS

Drug Name—Trade Name (representative)

Alprazolam—Xanax, Niravam
Bromazepam—Lexotan (Mex.)
Chlordiazepoxide—Librium
Clonazepam—Klonopin or Rivotril (Mex.)
Clorazepate—Tranzene
Diazepam—Valium
Estazolam—ProSom
Flunitrazepam—Rohypnol ("roofies")
Flurazepam—Dalmane
Halazepam—Paxipam
Lorazepam—Ativan
Midazolam—Versed
Nimetazepam—Erimin (Asian)
Nitrazepam—Mogadan
Oxazepam—Serax
Phenazepam—(Russian)
Prazepam—Centrax
Quazepam—Doral
Rohypnol—Flunitrazepam
Temazepam—Restoril
Triazolam—Halcion

Visual Description

Various tablets; may be ground up for snorting. Used to dose others for rape or robbery; may be powder or dissolved into liquid (in small vial or nasal spray or eye drop container).

Methods of Use

Ingested, Injected, Rectally, Snorted

Primary Symptoms of Use

Benzodiazepine drugs give a wide range of typical CNS depressant effects. Typically used as anti-anxiety tranquilizers, sleep aids, withdrawal treatment for other drugs, seizure medications, etc. Causes sedation, blurred vision, drowsiness, lethargy, ataxia, fatigue, mental depression, loss of coordination, hypotension, diminished reflexes, confusion, coma, etc. Hypothermia possible.

Special Testing Note

Some of these drugs are difficult to capture in testing. Some may not show up in a drug "screen" and require further testing. Triazolam and prazepam are particularly difficult to detect. Newer benzodiazepines or low concentrations may not be detected.

Additional Comments

Flunitrazepam (Rohypnol) and bromazepam (Lexotan) are not approved for use in the United States but are commonly smuggled into the U.S. for abuse purposes, especially from Mexico. Foreign prescriptions for flunitrazepam are not honored in the U.S.

COMBINATIONS

Drug Name—Trade Name

Chlordiazepoxide—Limbitrol
Chlordiazepoxide Hydrochloride in combination with **Clidinium Bromide**—Librax
Perphenazine in combination with **Amitriptyline Hydrochloride**—Triavil

Methods of use

Ingested (swallowing)

Purpose

Used to combine varying onsets and durations of sedation and to treat a combination of psychological disorders

ANTI-DEPRESSANTS

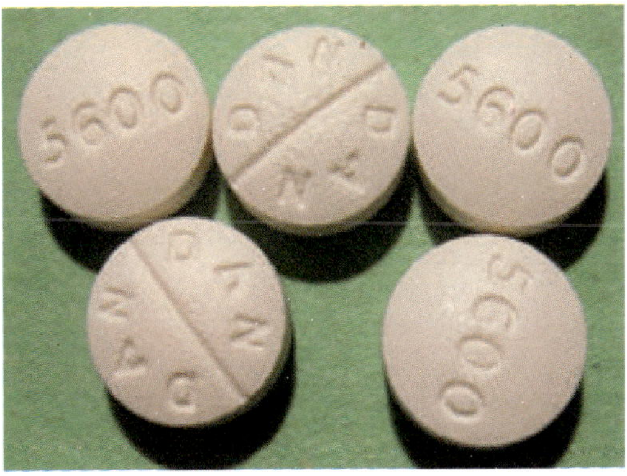

Trazadone (Desyrel)

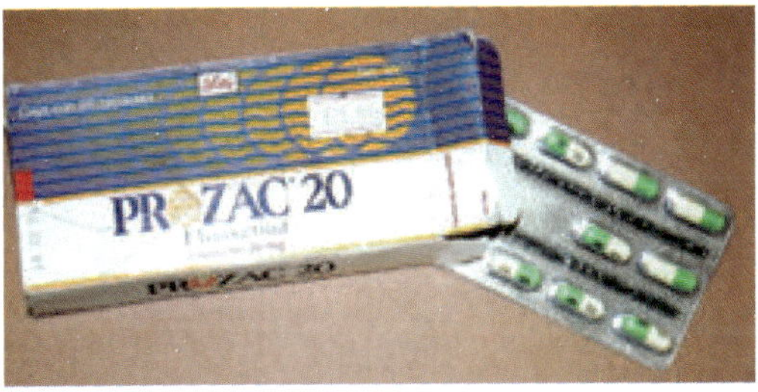

Fluoxetine (Prozac)

Continued on the next page.

ANTI-DEPRESSANTS

Drug Name—Trade Name (representative)

Amitriptyline HCl—Elavil
Amoxapine—Asendin
Bupropion—Wellbutrin, Zyban
Citalopram HCl—Celexa
Clomipramine—Anafranil
Desipramine: Norpramine
Doxepin HCl—Sinequan
Escitalopram—Lexapro
Fluoxetine—Prozac
Fluvoxamine—Luvox
Imipramine—Rofranil
Isocarboxazide—Marplan
Maprotiline—Ludiomil
Mirtazapine—Remeron
Nefazodone—Serzone
Nortriptyline—Aventyl or Pamelor
Paroxetine—Paxil
Phenelzine—Nardil
Protryptaline—Vivactil, Triptil (Canada)
Sertraline HCl—Zoloft
Tranylcypromine—Pamate
Trazadone—Desyrel
Trimipramine—Surmontil, Apo-Trimip (Canada)
Venlafaxine—Effexor

Visual Description

Various

Methods of Use

Ingested, Injected, Snorted

Primary Symptoms of Use

Can produce restlessness, anxiety and agitation, especially Bupropion. Mirtazapine (Remeron) has a prominent sedative effect. Overdose may cause ataxia, sedation, seizures, coma.

Additional Comments

Noncyclic anti-depressants such as Desyrel, Serzone, Prozac, Zoloft, Paxil, Luvox, Effexor and Wellbutrin, are typically less toxic than the tricyclics, such as Elavil, Asendin, Anafranil, Sinequan, Rofranil, Ludiomil, Aventyl, etc. Tricyclics are sometimes used in suicidal overdoses and represent a significant cause of poisoning in hospitalizations and deaths.

These drugs are listed in the DEPRESSANTS category based on their overall action of depressing the body's central nervous system. The term "anti-depressants" refers to the action of the drugs in adjusting the user's mental mood. The FDA now requires most anti-depressant medications to warn that these drugs may increase risks of suicidal thinking and behavior, especially in young adults during the first few months of treatment.

GHB/XYREM/GBL/BD/OTHER ANALOGS

(Depressant/Dissociative Anesthetic)

Visual Description

Commonly liquid, various textures; clear or yellowish color. Often colored for disguise or to avoid accidental consumption. No distinguishing odor—from mild chemical odor to nasty smell. Salty taste, but masked by sweet/fruity drinks. May see powder or capsules. Hydroscopic—likely to become moist if exposed to damp air.

Methods of Use

Ingested. Reported rectal insertion of GHB-soaked tampons, called "teabagging."

Duration of Effects

Onset: 10–20 minutes (some analogs slightly slower)
Duration: 3–5 hours

Primary Symptoms of Use

Nystagmus: Yes
Lack of Convergence: Yes
Pulse: Low
Pupils: Normal/May Be Dilated
Pupillary Reaction To Light: Slow
Blood Pressure: Low
Body Temperature: Near Normal to Low

Other Symptoms

Dizziness
Lack of facial expression (blank stare)
Droopy eyelids (Ptosis)
Amnesia
Vomiting/nausea
Aggression/combativeness or sexual stimulation possible
Drunken behavior (without odor of alcohol)
Muscle tone from flaccid to periods of rigidity
Sudden resolution of symptoms (after approx 4 hours)

Overdose Symptoms

Loss of bowel and urinary control Pulmonary edema
Cold & clammy skin Death
Coma
Shallow respiration (may drop to only 5–6 times per minute)
Special Testing Issues:
GHB is in blood 3–5 hours and urine approximately 12 hours

Associated Chemical/Analog Names

Gamma hydroxybutyrate (GHB); gamma butyrolactone (GBL); 1,4 butanediol (BD or BDO); pyrrolidone; gamma valerolactone (GVL); gamma hydroxyvalerate (GHV); octanediol; tetrahydrofuranone; tetramethylene glycol.

Continued on the next page.

GHB/XYREM/GBL/BD/OTHER ANALOGS

(Depressant/Dissociative Anesthetic)

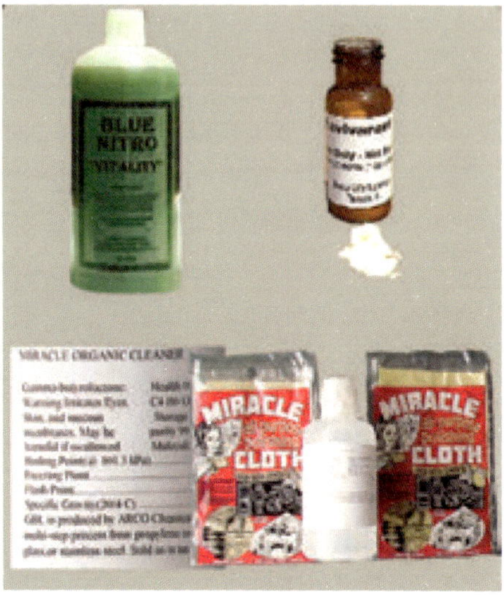

Miscellaneous forms of GBL.

GBL packaged as nail polish remover.

GHB/XYREM/GBL/BD/OTHER ANALOGS

(Depressant/Dissociative Anesthetic)

GHB Analogs

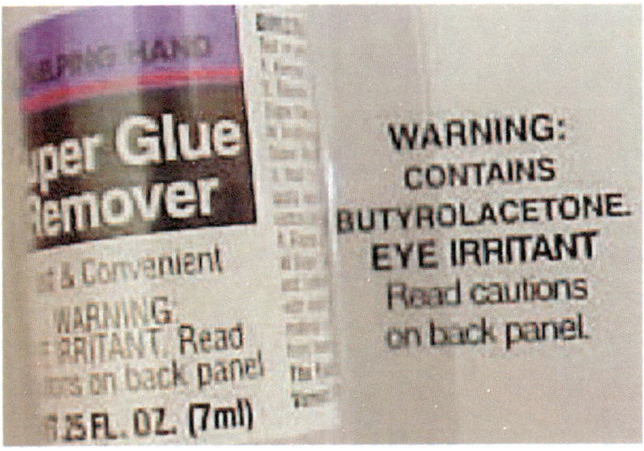

GBL "Super Glue Remover"

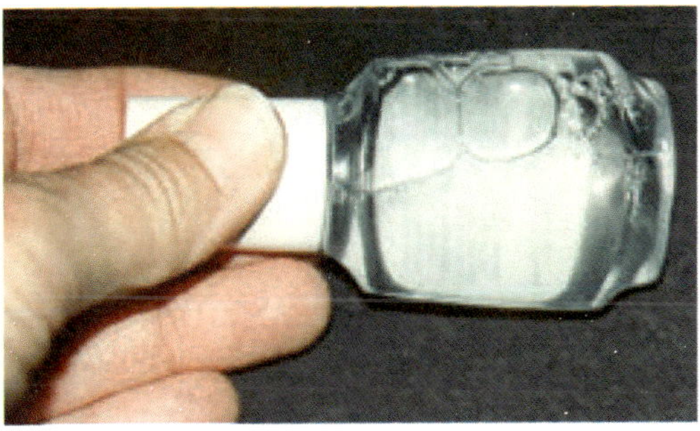

GHB "Mouthwash"

Continued on the next page.

GHB/XYREM/GBL/BD/OTHER ANALOGS

(Depressant/Dissociative Anesthetic)

GHB "Somax"

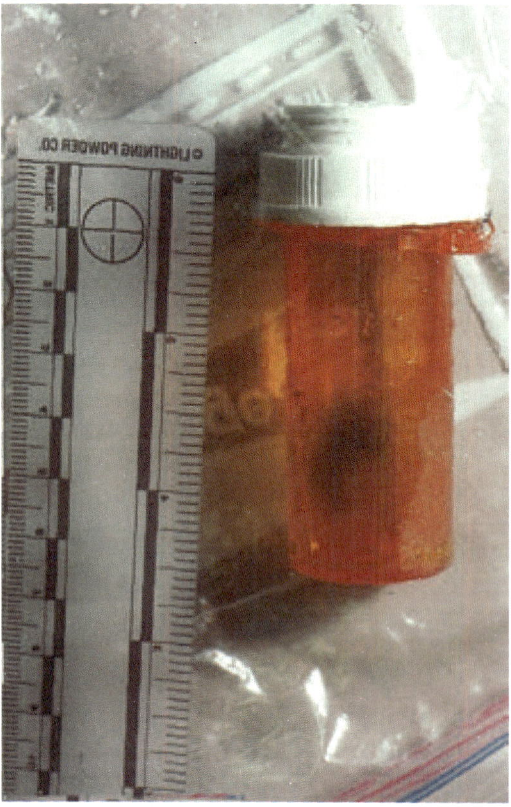

GHB packaged as evidence.

HALLUCINOGENS

PHENETHYLAMINES

2C-B—4-bromo-2,5-dimethoxyphenethylamine (Bromo, Nexus)
2C-E – 2,5 dimethoxy-4-ethylphenethylamine
2C-I – 2,5-dimethoxy-4-iodophenethylamine
2C-T-7 – 2,5-dimethoxy-4-(n)-propylthiophenethylamine (Lucky 7, Tripstacy)
2-TOM – 5-methoxy-4-methyl-2-methylthioamphetamine
3C-BZ—4-benzyloxy-3,5-dimethoxyamphetamine
3C-E – 3,5-dimethoxy-4-ethoxyamphetamine
5-TOM—2-methoxy-4-methyl-5-methylthio-A
DOB—4-bromo-2,5-dimethoxyamphetamine
DOC—4-chloro-2,5-dimethoxyamphetamine (analog of DOB)
MDA – 3,4 methylenedioxy-amphetamine
MDMA – 3,4 methylenedioxy-methamphetamine (See MDMA, Ecstasy, page 40)

Additional Comments

There are at least 179 drugs in the category. 2C-B and 2C-I are the most common, after MDMA and MDA. But there are others such as: 2C-C, 2C-D, 2C-E, 2C-G, 2C-G-5, 2C-N, 2C-P, 2C-T, 2C-T-2, 2C-T-4, 2C-T-5, 2C-T-8, 2C-T-9, 3C-BZ, 2–4-DMA, DOM, HOT-2, 4-MA, MDDM, MDBZ,MDMC, MEDA,MMDA, 4-TIM, TMA-4, 4-T-TRIS

Visual Description

Powder or pills, various colors and shapes; with or without logo imprints; DOC & DOB also seen as liquid in vials and blotter paper, resembling LSD format

Methods of Use

Ingested primarily as pills. May be snorted, crushed and put into a marijuana blunt for smoking, injected or inserted rectally (often called "booty bumping" or "plugging").

Duration of Effects

Varies greatly with the substance taken

Primary Symptoms of Use

Pupils: Dilated
Pulse: Elevated
Blood Pressure: Elevated
Body Temperature: Elevated

These drugs are generally hallucinogenic stimulants but with varying effects. Some are more hallucinogenic and some are more stimulant oriented. The effects will be somewhat similar to both categories.

Familiarity with this class of drugs is rather limited. Law enforcement, and even medical professionals, often have to refer to www.erowid.org for information about usage and effects. Much of the material on that pro-drug website is obtained from Dr. Alex Shulgin, known as "Papa Ecstasy", who created many of these drugs and has taken and documented all of them as well. A wider variety of these drugs is showing up with increasing frequency. Many are currently scheduled but many are not. Some may be covered as analogs of scheduled drugs. Contact your crime lab or DEA for the legal status in your state.

MDMA—PHENETHYLAMINES

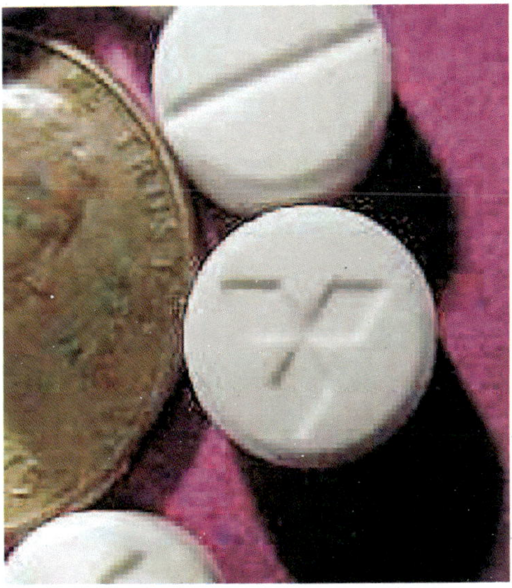

"Mitsubishi" MDMA (shown with penny for size comparison)

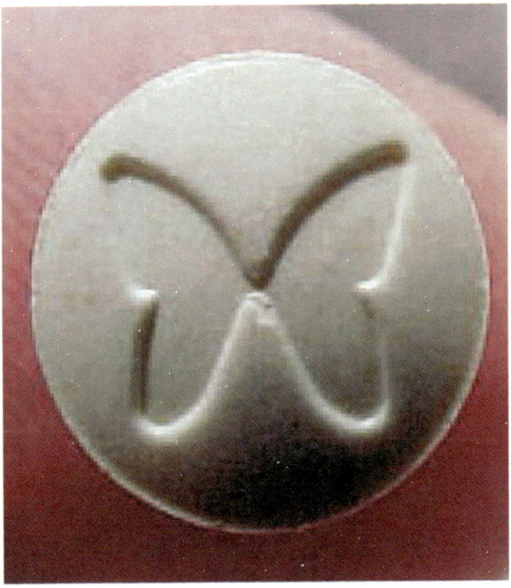

MDMA Fake

Actually Remifeminin, a harmless dietary supplement that happens to have a butterfly imprint and has been seen sold as Ecstasy. This product has the butterfly on both sides, rare for an actual MDMA pill.

Continued on the next page.

MDMA—PHENETHYLAMINES

MDMA with Calvin Klein "brand"

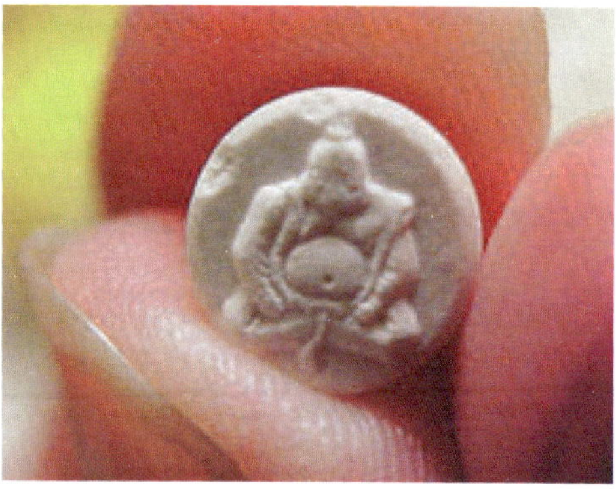

MDMA "Budda"

MDMA "Green Clover"

MDMA—PHENETHYLAMINES

MDMA Capsules

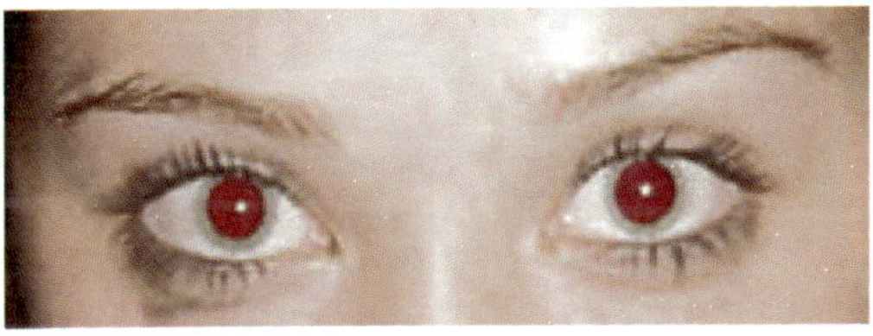

MDMA User (Note extremely dilated pupils)

Continued on the next page.

MDMA—PHENETHYLAMINES

MDMA — 3,4 METHYLENEDIOXYMETHAMPHETAMINE (Ecstasy, X, XTC, E, The Hug Drug)

MDA – 3,4 METHYLENEDIOXY-AMPHETAMINE (Phenethylamine)

Visual Description

White or off-white powder or pills. Pills may appear professionally pressed or coarse, homemade. May be a variety of shapes and colors. Seen plain (no logo) or any of 600 cartoons characters, business logos (Mitsubishi, Nike, etc), or symbols (heart, happy face, etc.) Price of a pill varies from $15 to $40; wholesale $6 to $9. (See Paraphernalia, page 153)

Methods of Use

Ingested primarily as pills. May be snorted, injected or inserted rectally.

Duration of Effects

Onset: 25–40 minutes
Duration: 4–6 hours desired effects
Impaired for driving up to 12 hours: may have intense fatigue afterwards.

Primary Symptoms of Use

Nystagmus: No
Lack of Convergence: No
Pulse: Elevated
Pupils: Dilated
Pupillary Reaction to Light: Minimal
Blood Pressure: Elevated
Body Temperature: High

Other Symptoms

Altered perception (visual alterations; true hallucinations not likely); altered sense of time.
Anxiety
Blurred vision
Bruxism
Chills or sweating
Decreased aggression (unless used poly drug or in high doses)
Depression (after effects wear off or with long-term use)
Dry mouth
Enhanced sense of smell, touch, taste, sight
Enhanced energy; hyperactive
Euphoria
Faintness
Greater self esteem (temporary)
Increased communication (talkative and open)
Lack of inhibitions
Nausea
Paranoia
Sensation of loving all and being loved by all
Sweating

MDMA—PHENETHYLAMINES

Overdose Symptoms

Body temperature out of control
Bizarre behavior
Coma
Psychosis
Death

Additional Comments

"Ecstasy" has become virtually an umbrella term for a variety of substances in that pills sold as such may contain little or no MDMA (Ecstasy). Related substances (see pages on tryptamines and phenethylamines) may be substituted or included in the pill content. Or the pill may contain meth (for stimulant effect) and LSD or PCP or mescaline (to provide hallucinogenic effect) to simulate MDMA. Or the pill may contain over-the-counter substances such as dextromethorphan (DXM, cough suppressant), ephedrine, or simply no active ingredient at all. The content of MDMA in actual MDMA pills may vary from 50 to 175 mg (typical pill size is around 300 mg). Key ingredient for MDMA is safrole (iso-safrole, bromo-safrole or chloro-safrole).

MDA provides more visual disturbance than MDMA and isn't quite as popular. Many of the pills sold as Ecstasy contain only MDA or MDA mixed with other drugs. It should be noted that MDA is also a breakdown product of MDMA in the body. Toxicology results may show a ratio of MDMA to MDA as roughly 85 to 15. That does not in itself indicate ingestion of MDA, but rather ingestion of MDMA metabolizing.

There are more than 600 recognized logos on Ecstasy pills, cartoon characters, business logos, letters, etc. Thus there are many nicknames, typically based on the logo and color or shape of the pill. They do not symbolize a particular dealer or maker. One pill press can produce a variety of logos daily as the metal die with the logo imprint can be readily changed through a pill run.

Death from heatstroke type of event can occur. Users dehydrate and are trained to drink large amounts of water, but excessive water intake during this period can also result in death from hyponatremia, water poisoning.

TRYPTAMINES

DMT in Foil Bindles

TRYPTAMINES

AMT—Alpha-methyl-tryptamine or Spirals, Amtrak or Amthrax

5-MeO-DIPT—5-methoxy-N,N-diisopropyltryptamine or Foxy or Foxy Methoxy

DMT—Dimethyltryptamine (DMT photo on previous page)

There are at least 55 drugs in this category. Most tryptamines occur in nature but all are also synthetically produced. Tryptamines include: 2-Me-DET, 2-Me-DMT, 4-MeO-DIPT, 4-HO-MIPT, 4-HO-DBT, 5-MeO-DMT, DIPT, MBT, 4,5-MDO-DIPT, MBT, AET, DET (analog of DMT)

Tryptamines commonly recognized as drugs of abuse (but perhaps not commonly known as tryptamines) include Psilocybin (O-phosphoryl-4-hydroxy-N,N-dimethyltryptamine) and psilocyn (4-hydroxy-N, N-dimethyltryptamine) and even LSD.

Visual Description

Powder or pills, various colors and shapes; with or without logo imprints. AMT is often seen in pills with the oval alien face or spider imprint. Foxy has been found in off-white or orange crystal powder or in capsule or tablet form.

Methods of Use

Ingested primarily as pills. May be snorted, injected, inserted rectally or smoked.

Duration of Effects

Varies greatly with the substance taken. AMT lasts 12–24 hours.
Foxy 3–6 hours.

Primary Symptoms of Use

Pupils: Dilated
Pulse: Elevated
Blood Pressure: Elevated
Body Temperature: Elevated

Other Symptoms

Visual and auditory distortions
Emotional disturbances

These drugs are hallucinogenic stimulants but with varying effects. Some are more hallucinogenic and some are more stimulant oriented. The effects will be somewhat similar to both categories.

Additional Comments

Familiarity with this class of drugs is rather limited. Law enforcement and even medical professionals often have to refer to erowid.org for information about usage and effects. Much of the material on that pro-drug website is obtained from Dr. Alex Shulgin, known as "Papa Ecstasy", who created many of these drugs and has taken and documented all of them as well.

Continued on the next page.

TRYPTAMINES

DMT (DIMETHYLTRYPTAMINE), also known as the "Businessman's Lunch" is one of the most commonly abused tryptamines. It is commonly found in crystalline form, powder or oil, and varies from white to pink to red, w/smell when heated similar to burning plastic.

DMT May be snorted, smoked as vapor or mixed with tobacco, marijuana, etc. and smoked, injected, and the effects last approximately 45–60 minutes

Primary Symptoms of Use

Horizontal Gaze Nystagmus: Not Present
Vertical Gaze Nystagmus: Not Present
Lack of Convergence: Not Present
Romberg Stand: Fast
Pulse: Fast
Pupils: Dilated
Pupillary Reaction To Light: Slow/Minimal

Other Symptoms

Blank stare
Body tremors
Dazed
Disoriented
Flashbacks
Hallucinations
Memory loss
Mood changes
Muscle tension
Nausea
Perspiring
Sleeplessness
Synesthesia

Overdose Symptoms

Bizarre behavior
Long, intense trips
Psychosis
Death

Additional Comments

5-MeO-DMT (5-methoxy-N,N-dimethyl- tryptamine) is related to DMT and comes from certain plants or is synthesized. Smoked or snorted. It is one of the two ingredients excreted by the Bufo Alvarius toad (indigenous to southwestern areas of U.S.). This toad excretes venom from glands on its back, containing hallucinogenic substances bufotenine and 5-MeO-DMT. Collected by squeezing the glands; smoke the dried extract. Popularized by the media as licking the toad's back (scaring it first to cause excretion). A wider variety of these drugs is showing up with increasing frequency. Many are currently scheduled, but many are not. Some may be covered as analogs of scheduled drugs. Contact your crime lab or DEA for the legal status in your state.

This page intentionally left blank.

JIMSON WEED
Datura

Jimson Weed Plant

Jimson Weed Growing Wild

Jimson Weed Pod and Seeds

JIMSON WEED
Datura

Visual Description
Green bush with white trumpet shaped flowers (can range white to purple). The flower pods contain seeds that are consumed. When dried, the pods are light green in color and prickly.

Methods of Use
Eaten or ingested as tea or smoked

Duration of Effects
Variable

Primary Symptoms of Use
Nystagmus: No
Pupils: Dilated
Pulse: Elevated
Blood Pressure: Elevated
Body Temperature: Elevated
Lack of Convergence: No

Other Symptoms
Blank stare
Body tremors
Delirium
Disoriented
Hallucinations
Impaired divided attention
Mood changes
Memory loss
Muscle tension
Nausea
Perspiring
Sleeplessness
Synesthesia

Overdose Symptoms
Bizarre behavior
Psychosis
Violence
Death

Additional Comments
Also called angel's trumpet, devil's trumpet, moon flower and Jamestown weed. Active ingredients are the alkaloids hyoscyamine, scopolamine and atropine. Can be very toxic and resulting behavior can be very dangerous.

LSD

Lysergic Acid Diethylamide

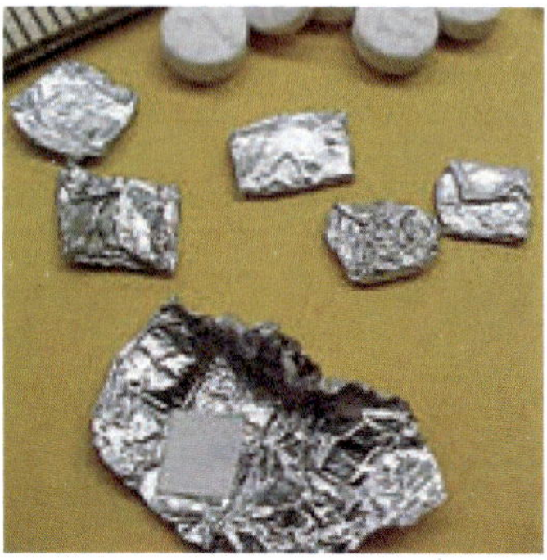

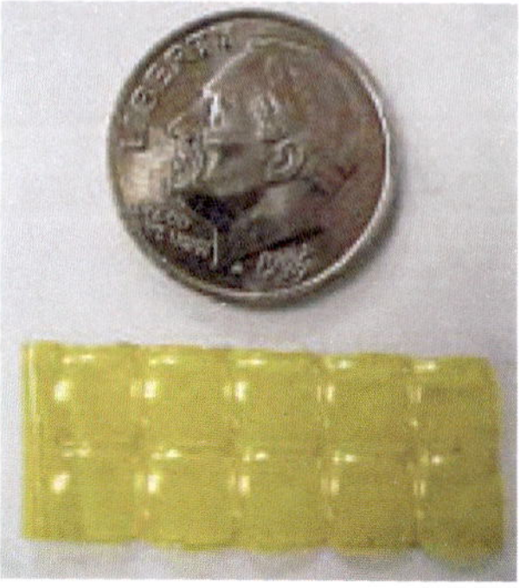

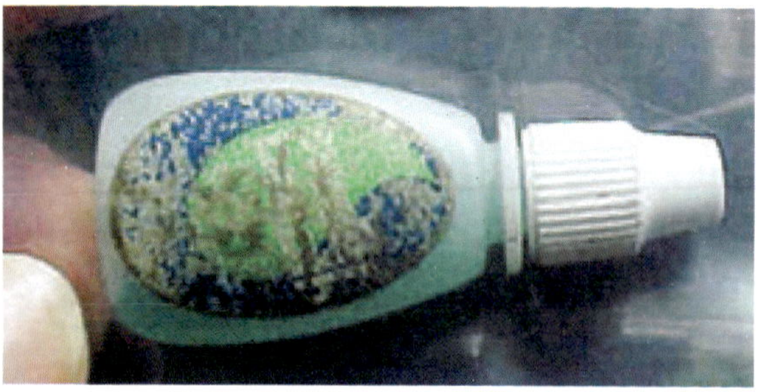

Various forms of LSD

LSD

Lysergic Acid Diethylamide

Visual Description

Varies—Pure crystals typically clear or white; traditional blotter paper (small squares, perforated sheets, or strips of impregnated paper, often with cartoon characters or artistic designs); on a sugar cube; often seen as a liquid (in small vials such as breath mint, eye or nasal spray, food coloring containers); in gel form as dots on plastic pieces that are sucked; gel form as "pyramids" on, or peeled from, fluorescent light diffuser plastic (used as a mold and then peeled off and cut into strips or perforated first, broken into pieces and sucked). May also be mixed in tablets sold as "Ecstasy" (may contain meth and LSD, if actual MDMA isn't available to achieve similar effects of hallucinogenic stimulant).

Methods of Use

Ingested; absorbed (skin contact or eye drops). Tiny quantities when in crystalline form (50 micrograms = one hit). Cannot be smoked (destroyed by heat). One ounce of pure LSD equals 567,000 hits, calculated at 50 micrograms each.

Duration of Effects

Onset: 20–60 minutes
Duration: 6–12 hours

Primary Symptoms of Use

Nystagmus: No
Pupils: Dilated
Pulse: Elevated
Blood Pressure: Elevated
Body Temperature: Elevated
Lack of Convergence: No

Other Symptoms

Anxiety (bad trip)
Ataxia
Blank stare
Dazed, disoriented, delirium
Fear & paranoia (bad trip)
Flashbacks
Hyperthermia (overheating)
Impaired sense of time & distance
Increased salivation
Impaired divided attention
Muscle tension
Nausea
Perspiring
Piloerection (goosebumps)
Psychosis
Synesthesia
Sleeplessness

Additional Comments

Synesthesia is a condition where one type of stimulation evokes the sensation of another, as when the hearing of a sound produces the visualization of a color.

LSA

D-Lysergic Acid Amide

Morning Glory Seeds, Hawaiian Woodrose Seeds

Close-up of Morning Glory Seeds

LSA

D-Lysergic Acid Amide

Visual Description

Seeds from Morning Glory (produces variety of flower colors), Hawaiian Woodrose, and Stipa robusta plants, plus ergot fungus.

Methods of Use

Suck on or swallow seeds.
Grind and soak the seeds and drink the liquid.
Brew tea.

Duration of Effects & Primary Symptoms of Use

See LSD; LSA provides similar effects though typically milder.

Additional Comments

This chemical is used in synthesizing LSD. Gives a milder version of an LSD trip.

PEYOTE

Peyote Cactus—Mescaline

Peyote Button

Peyote Flower

Peyote in Capsule Form

PEYOTE

Peyote Cactus—Mescaline

Visual Description

Capsules (gelatin capsules of ground plant material or white crystalline powder if synthesized), needle-shaped translucent crystals, hard brown discs of plant material (the "button" from the plant is removed and dried), tablets.

Methods of Use

Ingested as capsules or tablets or in soup or tea form; chewed; smoked.

Duration of Effects:

Onset: 30–60 minutes

Duration: 10–12 hours

Primary Symptoms of Use

Nystagmus: No

Pupils: Dilated

Pulse: Elevated

Blood Pressure: Elevated

Body Temperature: Elevated

Lack of Convergence: No

Other Symptoms

Ataxia

Dazed/disoriented

Hallucinations

Memory loss

Psychosis

Rancid breath

Synesthesia

Sweating

Nausea/vomiting

Additional Comments

Not illegal for certain members of the Native American Church; used for religious purposes. Documentation of tribal membership and authorization may be required for possession and transportation; verify requirements and department policy in your region.

PSILOCYBIN & PSILOCIN
(Magic Mushrooms)

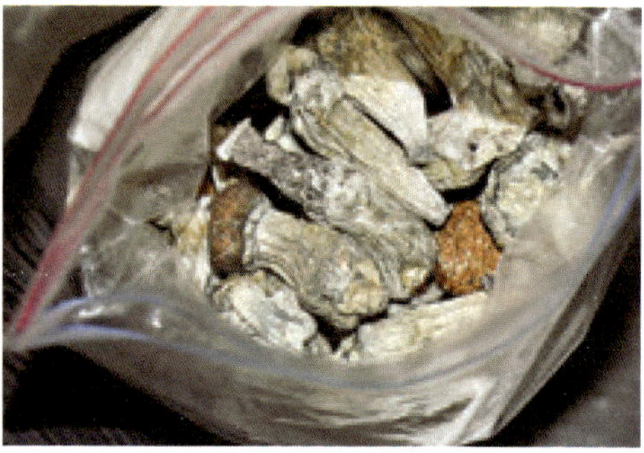

PSILOCYBIN & PSILOCIN
(Magic Mushrooms)

Visual Description
Fresh or dried mushrooms (only specific plants); white to brown powder or capsules. Usually stored dry to avoid mold and spoiling.

Methods of Use
Chewed as plant material, swallowed as a capsule or consumed as tea, ground and smoked mixed with marijuana

Duration of Effects
Onset: within 20 minutes
Duration: 6–12 Hours

Primary Symptoms of Use
Nystagmus: No
Pupils: Dilated
Pulse: Elevated
Blood Pressure: Elevated
Body Temperature: Elevated
Lack of Convergence: No

Other Symptoms
Abdominal pain
Ataxia
Chills
Dazed/Disoriented Numbness of face, tongue or lips
Difficult/Tremulous speech
Dizziness
Euphoria
Fever & Flushing
Hallucinations
Hypertension
Impaired concentration & perception
Muscle tension & twitching
Nausea
Psychosis
Sleeplessness
Slowed passage of time
Synesthesia
Urinary incontinence
Visualization of patterns with eyes closed
Vomiting

Additional Comments
Growing magic mushrooms for profit is typically a very high-tech operation with growing beds, elaborate conditions, sterilized fertilizer material, etc. Some mushrooms that may be mistaken for "magic mushrooms" are poisonous. Amanita muscaria mushrooms contain the substances ibotenic acid and muscimol (rather than psilocybin and psilocin), causing similar hallucinogenic reactions but may also be fatal. They have a brown, red or orange cap with white "warts."

SALVIA DIVINORUM

SALVIA DIVINORUM

Visual Description

Green plant material (seeds are uncommon; produced from plant cuttings most often). A sage type plant from the mint family. The active ingredient is Salvinorin A.

Methods of Use

Chewing leaves or drinking tea or soup concoction or smoking.
May mix with honey and eat by spoonfuls.

Duration of Effects

Onset: One minute
Peak: 5–10 minutes
Duration: One hour (Impairment for driving likely for several hours)

Primary Symptoms of Use

Nystagmus: No
Lack of Convergence: No
Pulse: Elevated
Pupils: Dilated
Pupillary Reaction to Light: Normal
Blood Pressure: Elevated
Body Temperature: High

Other Symptoms

Abdominal pain
Diarrhea
Difficulty communicating or unable
Euphoria
Hallucinations
Headache/Hangover
Intoxication
Meditative or trance state
Sweaty
Terrifying experiences possible
Uncontrolled laughter at onset
Vomiting
Visual disturbances

Additional Comments

The following states have placed limitations on the sale and/or possession of Salvia: Alabama, Alaska, Arkansas, California, Colorado, Connecticut, Delaware, Florida, Georgia, Illinois, Indiana, Iowa, Kansas, Kentucky, Louisiana, Maine, Maryland, Massachusetts, Michigan, Minnesota, Mississippi, Missouri, Nebraska, New Jersey, New York, North Carolina, North Dakota, Ohio, Oklahoma, Oregon, Pennsylvania, South Carolina, South Dakota, Tennessee, Texas, Utah, Virginia, Wisconsin and Wyoming. Some other countries have banned it as well. More hallucinogenic than marijuana and somewhat similar to ingestion of Datura (Jimson Weed), legislation is needed in every state. Sold under such names as "purple sticky," 10X, 20X, 30X, Happy-Smoke and Maria Pastora in head shops around the country and on the Internet.

NUTMEG—MYRISTICIN

3-Methoxy-4,5-methylene-dioxyallybenzene and Related Compounds

NUTMEG—MYRISTICIN

3-Methoxy-4,5-methylene-dioxyallybenzene and Related Compounds

Visual Description

Dried kernel of the myristica fragrans tree, ground for use as a spice.

Methods of Use

Ingested; usually mixed with liquid to avoid chewing. Some recommend trying to swallow it dry while others recommend orange juice and honey and other recommend frozen concoctions with ice and lemonade. Requires fairly large amounts, such as multiple tablespoons. One pro-drug website nutmeg user recommends 15 grams for a 150 pound person as a starting point, for example.

Duration of Effects

Onset: From 2 to 8 hours after ingestion
Duration: 24 hours, with minor effects up to 48–72 hours

Primary Symptoms of Use

Nystagmus: No
Lack of Convergence: No
Pulse: Elevated
Pupils: Dilated
Pupillary Reaction to Light: Normal
Blood Pressure: Elevated
Body Temperature: High

Other Symptoms

Ataxia
Constipation
Delirium
Diarrhea
Dry mouth
Euphoria
Flushing
Hallucinations
Hypothermia
Nausea
Psychosis
Sleepiness afterwards
Synesthesia
Tachycardia
Vomiting

Additional Comments

Though not illegal, nutmeg is often banned from correctional institution kitchens. Not widely abused due to more negative than positive effects, but accessible to youth who seek drug experience. Impairs the ability to drive a motor vehicle.

MISCELLANEOUS HALLUCINOGENIC STIMULANTS

Many of these more unusual drugs (TFMPP, BZP, Euphoria and some of the phenethylamines and tryptamines) are seen as powder or crystal form or may be found pressed into pills just like MDMA (Ecstasy) in appearance. The powders may be in nondescript baggies or in vials or bags labeled as "research chemicals."

MISCELLANEOUS HALLUCINOGENIC STIMULANTS

4-METHYLAMINOREX (AKA: Euphoria, U4EUH or "Ice")

Chemical name

4,5-dihydro-4-methyl-5-phenyl-2-oxazolamine

Duration of Effects

Onset: 1–2 hours
Duration: 14–16 hours

Primary Symptoms of Use

Intense stimulant with sensations of boundless energy and mental acuity. Enhanced sense of self-esteem. Described by some as a long-lasting MDMA intoxication superimposed with methamphetamine. Other effects: increased respiration, tachycardia, tremors, perspiration, increased blood pressure, intraocular pressure, blurred vision, tightness in the chest, increased body and breath odor. Has not become particularly popular, likely due to the excessiveness of its effects.

PIPERAZINES —BZP, TFMPP BENZYLPIPERAZINE (BZP)

Sold as a substitute for Ecstasy, MDMA, BZP is a stimulant with some expanded properties, somewhat similar to MDMA, but also with more undesirable side effects. BZP is federally scheduled. Known as "Poor Man's Ecstasy." Effects last 6–8 hours. Another piperazine surfaced in 2007. The chemical, 1-(chlorophenyl) piperazine (AKA: meta-chlorophenylpiperazine or mCPP) was the major component of pills resembling the usual MDMA pill format. The pills contained only traces of MDMA. BZP is federally scheduled.

TRIFLUOROMETHYLPHENYLPIPERAZINE (TFMPP)

Seen sometimes on its own or mixed with BZP and sold as a recreational drug that is a "legal alternative" to MDMA and/or LSD. Little is known about TFMPP effects. Like BZP it is a stimulant with additional properties. TFMPP is not federally scheduled and is sometimes sold as a legal alternative to LSD and MDMA. While BZP & TFMPP have been the common piperazines of abuse, others have been found in recent times. The piperazine 1-(3-chlorophenyl) piperazine, also known as meta-chlorophenyl piperazine or mCPP), appeared in pill format in a 2007 law enforcement seizure in Indiana. The piperazine 1(2-methoxyphenyl)-piperazine, or OMPP, appeared in a Texas seizure.

This page intentionally left blank.

INHALANTS

INHALANT ABUSE (GENERAL)

Two Common Inhalants

INHALANT ABUSE (GENERAL)

Four Categories of inhalants

Solvents—Toluene products, paint/paint thinner, lighter fluid, carburetor cleaner, dry cleaning fluid, correction fluid (some brands), household glue/cement, felt-tip markers, gasoline (benzene), kerosene, fingernail polish remover, grease/spot remover (methylene chloride and toluene)

Aerosols—Spray paint, deodorant, body sprays, room odorizer, hair spray, fabric protector, vegetable cooking spray

Gases—Butane, nitrous oxide and other medical anesthetics (ether, chloroform, halothane), propane, helium, freon

Nitrites—Amyl (some medical use: angina, for example), butyl nitrite (video head cleaner), cyclohexyl nitritem (Note: Nitrites are slightly different as they primarily dilate blood vessels and relax the muscles and thus are primarily used as sexual enhancers)

Visual Description

There are more than 1400 volatile, potentially abusable products on the market today, including hydrocarbons, nitrites, anesthetics, alcohols, and halogen compounds. They are called volatile organic compounds (VOC). They are products never meant for human consumption, such as butane, fabric protector, gasoline, spray paint, hair spray, marking pens, air fresheners, computer keyboard sprays, cleaning agents, starter fluid, fire extinguisher (halon) and glue. Some are inhaled for the named product itself (such as gasoline, glue) while others are abused for the propellant that releases the product (such as nitrous oxide that fires homemade whipped cream makers and propels whipped cream from store-bought cans and cardiac synthesizers that propel air freshener from their containers).

Methods of Use

Inhaled from a cloth or bag or balloon, or directly from the container

Duration of Effects

Onset: Rapid
Duration: Brief

Continued on the next page.

INHALANT ABUSE (GENERAL)

Primary Symptoms of Use (varies with substance)

Nystagmus: Yes
Lack of Convergence: Present
Pupils: Normal, But May Be Dilated
Pulse: Above Normal
Pupillary Reaction To Light: Normal To Slow

Other Symptoms

Acute confusion
Agitation
Ataxia
Brain Damage (especially with long-term use)
Brief euphoria
Cardiac arrhythmia/failure (especially with fluorocarbons)
Decrease in appetite
Headaches
Liver & kidney damage possible
Odor of substance
Poor memory
Shortness of breath/chest pains
Slurred speech
Stains on clothing or skin
Sores/rash around mouth/nose
Suicide risk (with persistent use)
Sullen/lethargic moods
Tremors
Vomiting

Overdose Symptoms

Coma
Death

Additional Comments

Long-term use can cause weight loss, fatigue, muscle fatigue. Consistent inhaling of vapors can, over time, permanently damage the nervous system. Inhaling while driving is particularly dangerous and has resulted in traffic accidents and deaths. Another indicator is hidden, excessive numbers of spray product containers, chemical-soaked rags or clothing. Testing is difficult due to the brief time period for most of these products.

This page intentionally left blank.

AMYL/BUTYL NITRITE, CYCLOHEXYL NITRITE

AMYL/BUTYL NITRITE, CYCLOHEXYL NITRITE

Visual Description

Packaged in small bottles, sold as room deodorizers, video head cleaner, etc. Often called "Locker Room," "Rush," "Come," "Brush," etc.

Methods of Use

Vapors Inhaled

Duration of Effects

Onset: Rapid
Duration: 2–5 minutes

Primary Symptoms of Use

Nystagmus: Yes
Lack of Convergence: Present
Pupils: Normal, But May Be Dilated
Pulse: Above Normal
Pupillary Reaction To Light: Normal To Slow

Other Symptoms

Confusion
Disoriented
Flushed head and neck
Headaches
Odor of substance
Slurred speech
Sudden "head rush"

Overdose Symptoms

Asphyxiation (buildup of inhaled fumes, displacing oxygen in lungs)
Coma
Death

Additional Comments

Long-term use can cause weight loss, fatigue, muscle fatigue. Consistent inhaling of vapors can, over time, permanently damage the nervous system. Amyl nitrite has legitimate medical use—angina, for example. Nitrites are slightly different than other inhalants as they primarily dilate blood vessels and relax the muscles (including the sphincter muscles) and thus are primarily used as sexual enhancers.

NITROUS OXIDE
(Laughing Gas, AKA: N2O; NOZ)

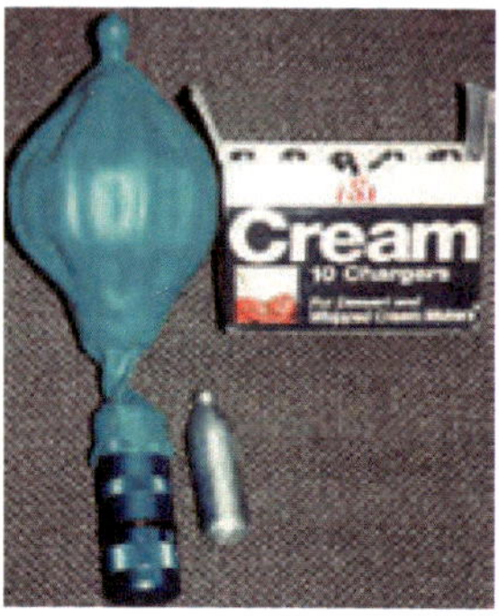

NOZ balloon with "cracker" & cartridges

Another form of legitimate NOZ tanks

NOZ tanks from Rave

NITROUS OXIDE

(Laughing Gas AKA: N20; NOZ)

Visual Description

Large dark blue tank (medical grade), medium size bright blue tank (vehicle/motorcycle racing performance enhancement), small metal cylinder (called "whip-its" or "whippets" –often mistaken for CO2 but slightly shorter and dull silver in color), whipped cream dispenser (spray down for whipped cream; point upward to release the nitrous oxide propellant). May be found with a facemask (to hook via hose to large tanks), balloons (heavier grade than common balloons), or a metal or plastic "cracker" (device to release the gas into balloons from the whip-its). Nitrous Oxide is particularly popular at all-night raves.

Methods of Use

Inhaled from balloon or tank

Duration of Effects

Onset: Rapid
Duration: Brief

Primary Symptoms of Use

Nystagmus: Yes
Lack of Convergence: Present
Pupils: Normal, But May Be Dilated
Pulse: Above Normal
Pupillary Reaction To Light: Normal To Slow

Other Symptoms

Anemia (chronic use)
Ataxia
Cardiac arrhythmia
Confusion
Dizziness
Disoriented
Euphoria (brief)
Injury due to falling (brief unconsciousness common)
Headache
Seizures
Slurred speech

Overdose Symptoms

Coma
Death

Additional Comments

Used in dental practices, nitrous oxide is delivered with a controlled amount of oxygen. Abused from balloons, face masks, etc., the experience is quite different. Oxygen deprivation is the main issue in acute toxicity from nitrous oxide abuse.

This page intentionally left blank.

NARCOTIC ANALGESICS AND OPIATES

CODEINE

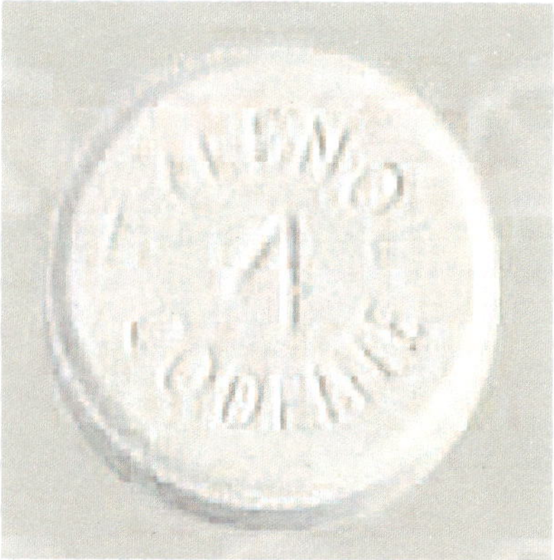

Tylenol® w/Codeine #4 (Brand name)

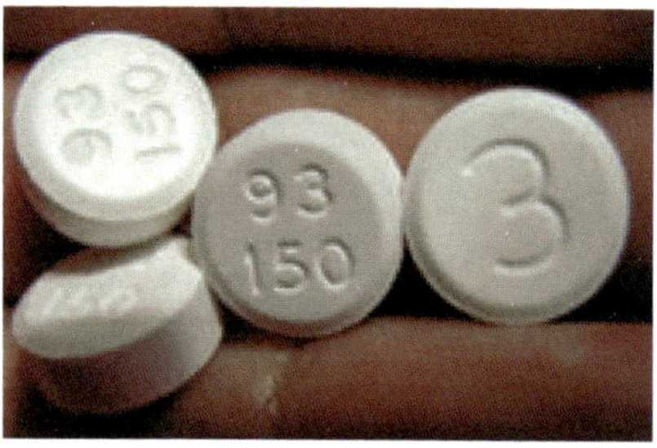

Acetaminophen w/Codeine #3 (Generic)

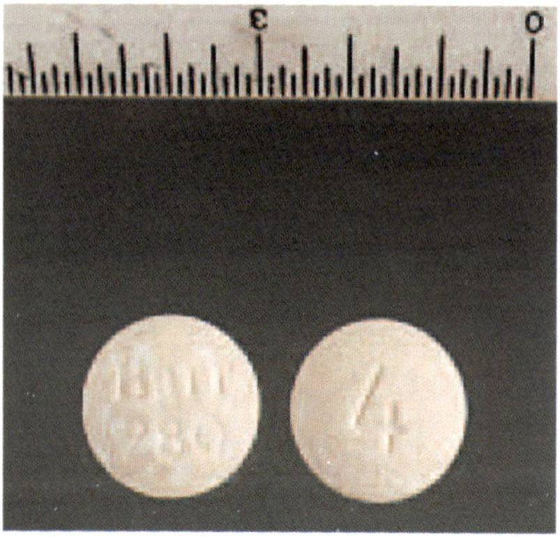

Aspirin w/Codeine #4 (Generic)

CODEINE

Trade Names & Combinations

Tylenol w/Codeine
APAP w/Codeine
Empirin w/Codeine
Codeine w/Promethazine
Robitussin A-C, Phenergan w/Codeine
Prometh w/Codeine
Fiorinal (butalbital) w/Codeine

Visual Description

Capsules, Dark Liquid (varying in thickness), Tablets

Methods of Use

Ingested, Injected, Snorted

Duration of Effects

Onset: 30–60 minutes (oral)
Peak: 1–1.5 hours (oral)
Loaded: 4–6 hours

Primary Symptoms of Use

Nystagmus: No
Lack of Convergence: No
Pulse: Below Normal
Pupils: Constricted
Pupillary Reaction to Light: Slow
Blood Pressure: Below Normal
Body Temperature: Normal/Below Normal

Other Symptoms

Depressed reflexes
Droopy eyelids (Ptosis)
Drowsiness
Dry mouth
Euphoria
Fresh puncture marks
Impaired divided attention
Low, raspy voice
Nausea
Poor muscle coordination
Profuse scratching
Vomiting

Overdose Symptoms

Blurred vision
Cold, clammy skin
Coma
Constipation
Convulsions
Death
Rapid, weak pulse
Slow, shallow breathing

Additional Comments

Tolerance to narcotics develops quickly, making drug dependence very likely. Phenergan w/codeine is a popular substance of abuse, popularized as "sipping syrup" in rap and hip-hop songs. The cough syrup may be consumed from a baby bottle.

FENTANYL

Fentanyl Patch

FENTANYL

Trade Names & Combinations

Actiq (lozenge lollipop)
Alfenta Innovar
Duragesic (patch)
Fentora (buccal tablet)
Sublimaze
Sufenta

Legitimate Fentanyl Derivatives

Alfentanyl
Fentanyl
Lofentanyl
Sufentanyl

Illicit Analogs

Alpha-methyl fentanyl
Benzyl fentanyl
3-methyl fentanyl

Visual Appearance

White/tan powder, liquid, patch (prescription), lollipop (lozenge on a stick), or tablet.

Methods of Use

Ingested, injected, snorted, sucked (Actiq format), or placed in mouth against gum, intended for gradual absorption (Fentora tablet format).

Duration of Effects

Onset: Rapid w/injection (slower with patch format)
Loaded: 30 minutes to 2 hours (longer in patch format)

Primary Symptoms of Use

Nystagmus: No
Lack of Convergence: No
Pulse: Below Normal
Pupils: Constricted
Pupillary Reaction To Light: Slow
Blood Pressure: Below Normal
Body Temperature: Normal/Below Normal

Other Symptoms

Depressed reflexes
Droopy eyelids (Ptosis)
Drowsiness
Dry mouth
Euphoria
Fresh puncture marks
Impaired divided attention
Nausea
Poor muscle coordination
Profuse scratching
Vomiting

Overdose Symptoms

Cold, clammy skin
Coma
Convulsions
Death
Rapid, weak pulse
Slow, shallow breathing

Additional Comments

Prescription patches contain a concentrated gel that is being extracted and abused. Use of full amount from patch is likely to be fatal, due to the high dose (intended for transdermal, ongoing transfer, not use all at once). **Wear gloves when handling open fentanyl patches.** In 1979 illicit derivatives of fentanyl began appearing in the streets as "China White," a name usually associated with the very pure Southeast Asian heroin.

HEROIN
Diacetylmorphine

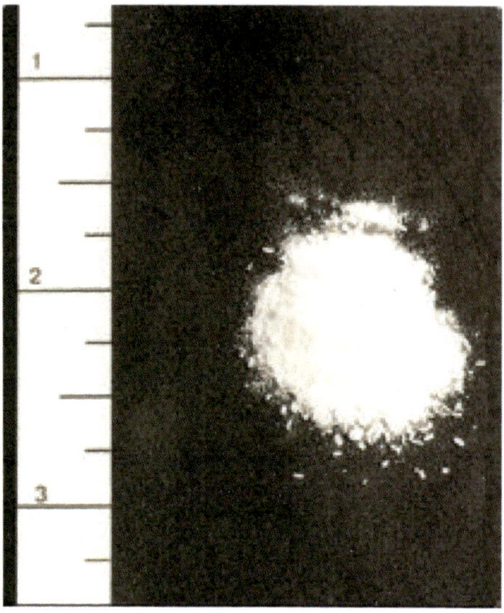

Asian-China White
(White powder)

Black Tar Heroin
(Black tar-like substance, has a vinegar odor)

HEROIN

Diacetylmorphine

Brown Heroin
(White or Light Brown Powder)

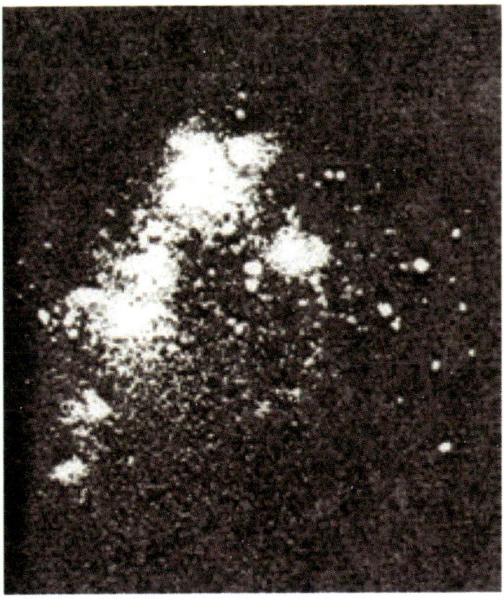

Columbian Heroin
(White powder)

Continued on the next page.

HEROIN

Diacetylmorphine

Heroin Balloon

Frequently a toy balloon is used to package Mexican Brown Powdered Heroin. The balloon is used to enable the possessor to swallow the balloon if approached by authorities. It is later retrieved after defecation.

HEROIN

Diacetylmorphine

Visual Description

White to beige or brown powdered substance; or black tar-like substance (chunks may resemble coal, with brown powder clinging to it). May have vinegar odor.

Methods of Use

Ingested, injected, snorted, smoked (black tar heroin)

Duration of Effects

Onset: Rapid; varies with route of administration. Intense euphoria 45 seconds to several minutes
Peak: 1–2 hours
Loaded: 3–4 hours (Addicts may inject 2–4 times daily)

Primary Symptoms of Use

Nystagmus: No
Lack of Convergence: No
Pulse: Below Normal
Pupils: Constricted
Pupillary Reaction To Light: Slow
Blood Pressure: Below Normal
Body Temperature: Normal/Below Normal

Other Symptoms

Depressed reflexes
Droopy eyelids (Ptosis)
Drowsiness
Dry mouth
Euphoria
Fresh puncture marks
Impaired divided attention
Low, raspy voice
Nausea
Poor muscle coordination
Profuse scratching
Vomiting

Overdose Symptoms

Cold, clammy skin
Coma
Convulsions
Delirium
Rapid, weak pulse
Slow, shallow breathing

Additional Comments

Tolerance to narcotics develops quickly making drug dependence very likely.

CHEESE
(Starter Heroin)

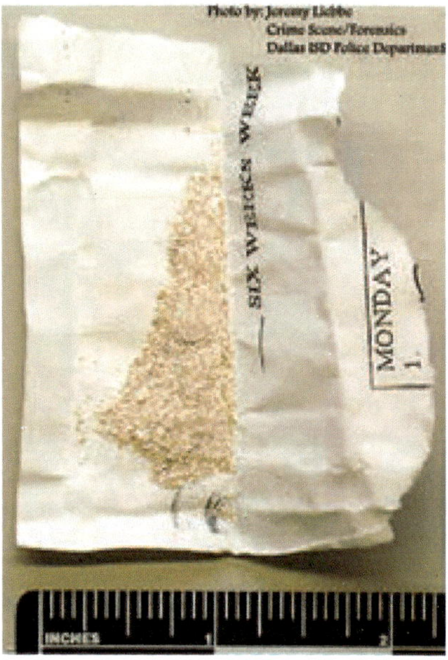

Cheese Powder

(Photo courtesy of Ofcr. Jeremy Liebbe, Dallas Independent School District)

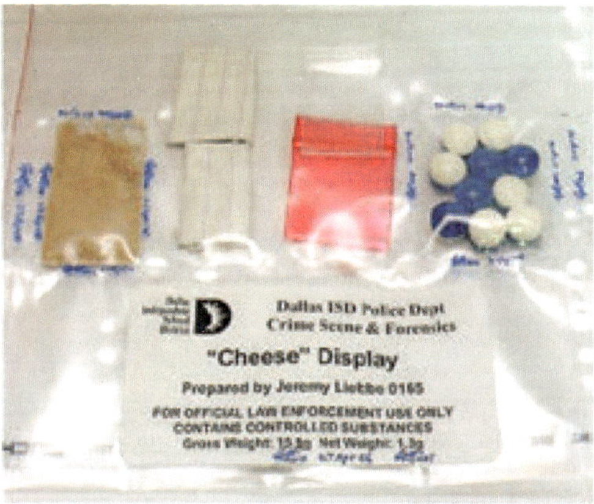

Display of Cheese powder, bindles and tablets

(Photo courtesy of Ofcr. Jeremy Liebbe, Dallas Independent School District)

CHEESE
(Starter Heroin)

Visual Description
Varying shades of coarse tan powder. May be found in small paper bindles or small zip-lock baggies. "Cheese" is a mixture of heroin (usually 8 percent or less) and diphenhydramine (ground up tablets of TylenolPM® or Benadryl®) as a way of introducing new users (typically teens) to heroin abuse.

Methods of Use
Usually snorted through straw, tube or lower half of small ink pens

Duration of Effects
Varies with dosage and frequency of doses
Diphenhydramine: 1–7 hours

Primary Symptoms of Use
Comparable to heroin
Ataxia
Drowsiness
Lethargy
Euphoria
Excessive thirst
Disorientation
Urinary retention

Withdrawal from Chronic Use
Mood swings
Insomnia
Headache
Nausea/vomiting
Bone pain
Muscle spasm

Overdose Symptoms
Increased heart rate
Decreased blood pressure
Delirium
Irritability
Double vision
Coma
Respiratory depression or arrest
Death

Additional Comments
This has been primarily a problem in the Dallas, Texas, area but there are reports Cheese has surfaced in other parts of the country. Focus has been on teens and especially Hispanic teens. Look for terms like Chees, Cheez, Chez, Chz, Queso, Keso, Kso in cell phone text messages and emails, for example.

HYDROMORPHONE
Dilaudid

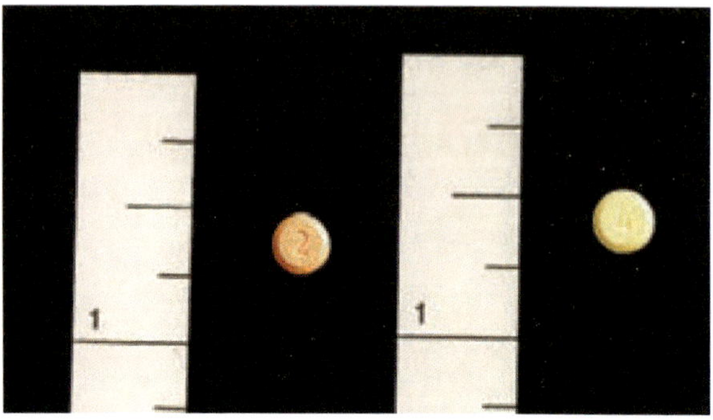

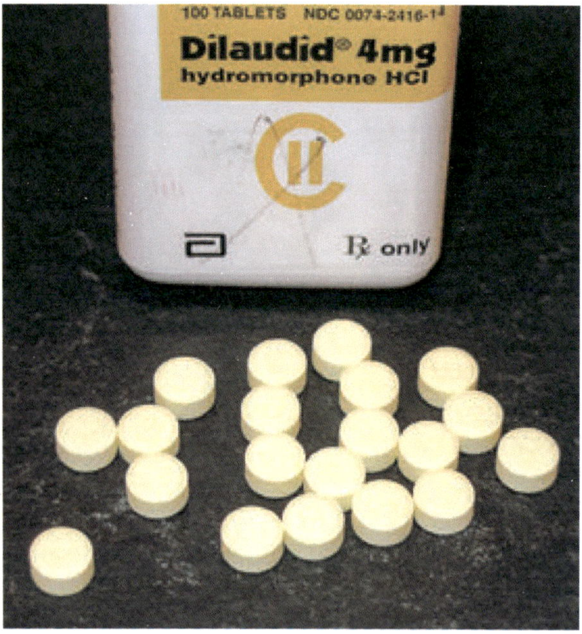

Dilaudid 4mg Tablets

HYDROMORPHONE
Dilaudid

Visual Description
Powder, pills (white, pink, orange, light green, yellow) 1–8 mg.

Methods of Use
Ingested, Injected or Snorted

Duration of Effects
Onset: 15–30 minutes
Peak: 30–60 minutes
Duration: 4–6 Hours

Primary Symptoms of Use
Nystagmus: No
Lack of Convergence: No
Pulse: Below Normal
Pupils: Constricted
Pupillary Reaction To Light: Slow
Blood Pressure: Below Normal
Body Temperature: Normal/Below Normal

Other Symptoms
Depressed reflexes
Droopy eyelids (Ptosis)
Drowsiness
Dry mouth
Euphoria
Fresh puncture marks
Impaired divided attention
Low, raspy voice
Nausea
Poor muscle coordination
Profuse scratching
Vomiting

Overdose Symptoms
Cold, clammy skin
Coma
Convulsions
Death
Rapid, weak pulse
Slow, shallow breathing

Additional Comments
Tolerance to narcotics develops quickly, making drug dependence very likely.

HYDROCODONE

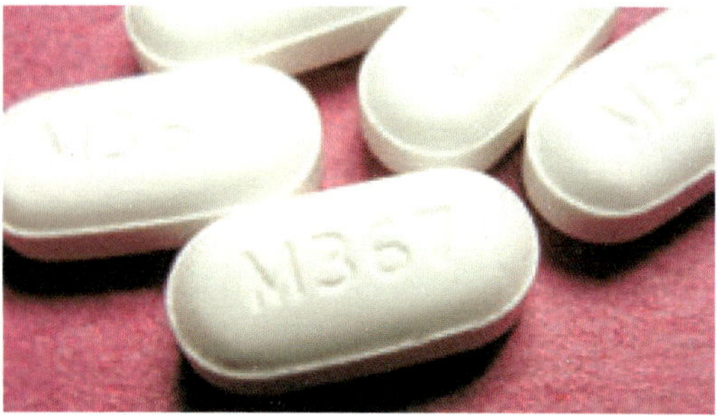

APAP / Hydrocodone

Vicodin (front)

Vicodin (back)

HYDROCODONE

Trade Names & Combinations

Hydrocodone & Acetaminophen—Vicodin, Lorcet, Lortab, Norco
Tussionex—cough syrup
Hydrocodone & Aspirin—Damason
Hydrocodone & Homatropine—Hycodan
Hydrocodone & Ibuprofen—Vicoprofen

Visual Description

Liquid, pills (oblong pills in white, light pink, bright pink, orange, yellow, light blue or red capsules), powder

Methods of Use

Ingested, injected, snorted

Duration of Effects

Loaded: 4–8 hours

Primary Symptoms of Use

Nystagmus: No
Lack of Convergence: No
Pulse: Below Normal
Pupils: Constricted
Pupillary Reaction To Light: Slow
Blood Pressure: Below Normal
Body Temperature: Normal/Below Normal

Other Symptoms

Depressed reflexes
Droopy eyelids (Ptosis)
Drowsiness
Dry mouth
Euphoria
Fresh puncture marks
Impaired divided attention
Low, raspy voice
Nausea
Poor muscle coordination
Profuse scratching
Vomiting

Overdose Symptoms

Cold, clammy skin
Coma
Convulsions
Death
Rapid, weak pulse
Slow, shallow breathing

Additional Comments

Hydrocodone products are a Schedule II drug and are easily diverted. When addicts cannot get more powerful drugs, they will settle for this and combine it with a CNS Depressant (such as Xanax or Klonopin).

MEPERIDINE

Meperidine Tabs

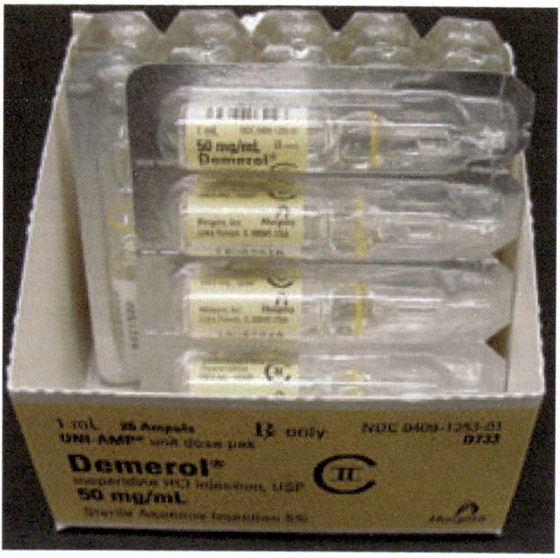

Demerol Unit Dose Injectable Vials

MEPERIDINE

Trade Names & Combinations

Demerol
Meperitab

Visual Description

Tablets (white, 50–100 mg), Clear Liquid, White Powder

Methods of Use

Ingested, Injected, Snorted

Duration of Effects

Onset: 10–15 minutes
Peak: 1 hour
Duration: 2–6 Hours

Primary Symptoms of Use

Nystagmus: No
Lack of Convergence: No
Pulse: Below Normal
Pupils: Constricted
Pupillary Reaction To Light: Slow
Blood Pressure: Below Normal
Body Temperature: Normal/Below Normal

Other Symptoms

Depressed reflexes
Droopy eyelids (Ptosis)
Drowsiness
Dry mouth
Euphoria
Fresh puncture marks
Impaired divided attention
Low, raspy voice
Nausea
Poor muscle coordination
Profuse scratching
Vomiting

Overdose Symptoms

Cold, clammy skin
Convulsions
Rapid, weak pulse
Slow, Shallow Breathing
Coma
Death

Additional Comments

Tolerance to narcotics develops quickly, making drug dependence very likely.

METHADONE
(AKA: Dolophine, Methadose)

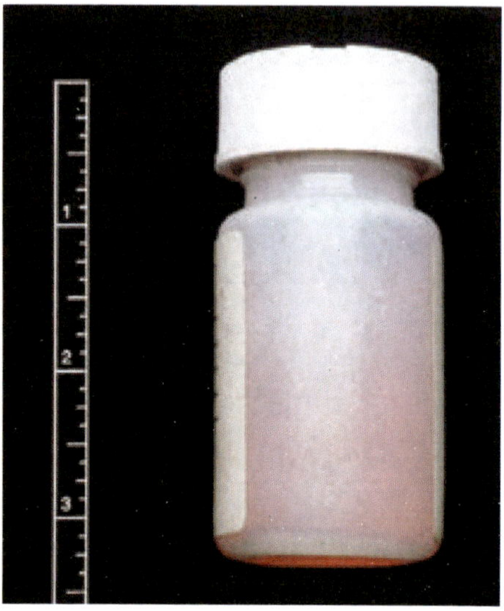

Methadone Liquid

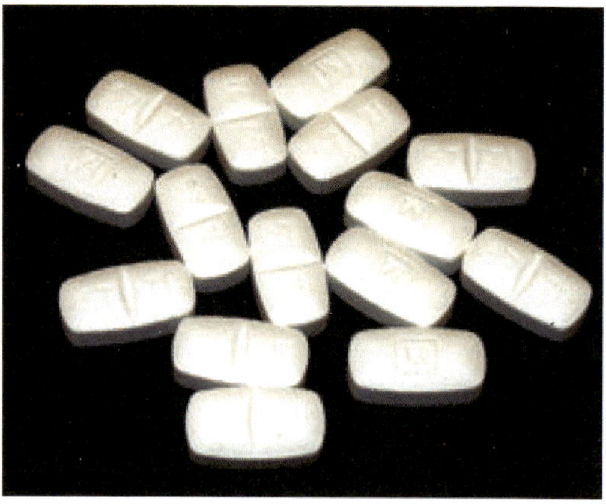

Methadone Tablets

METHADONE

(AKA: Dolophine, Methadose)

Trade Names

Dolophine
Methadose
Metadol (Canadian)

Visual Description

Clear, pink liquid or white or peach tablet, 5–40 mg

Methods of Use

Ingested, Injected, Snorted

Duration of Effects

Onset: 30–60 minutes
Duration: 4–8 Hours (w/repeated doses, increased to 22–24 hrs

Primary Symptoms of Use

Nystagmus: No
Lack of Convergence: No
Pulse: Below Normal
Pupils: Constricted
Pupillary Reaction To Light: Slow
Blood Pressure: Below Normal
Body Temperature: Normal/Below Normal

Other Symptoms

Depressed reflexes
Droopy eyelids (Ptosis)
Drowsiness
Dry mouth
Euphoria
Fresh puncture marks
Impaired divided attention
Low, raspy voice
Nausea
Poor motor coordination
Vomiting

Overdose Symptoms

Cold, clammy skin
Coma
Convulsions
Death
Rapid, weak pulse
Slow, shallow breathing

Additional Comments

When taken in proper doses, methadone should not show any effects. It is used to keep the heroin addict "well" and reduce the craving for heroin. They remain addicted to the opioid, but methadone blocks the high from heroin and does not provide a euphoric rush. It is only effective in cases of addiction to heroin, morphine, and other opioid drugs; it is not an effective treatment for other drugs of abuse. Law enforcement officers are typically familiar only with the use of methadone in heroin addiction treatment. In fact, it is also a pain medication being increasingly widely used by doctors to treat pain and thus even more widely abused. Methadone stays in the system a long time, meaning it can build up and can reach toxic levels. Deaths from methadone overdose have been increasing.

MORPHINE

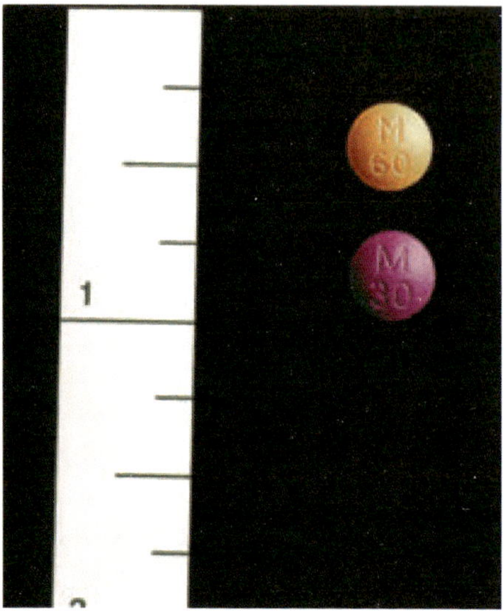

Morphine Tablets

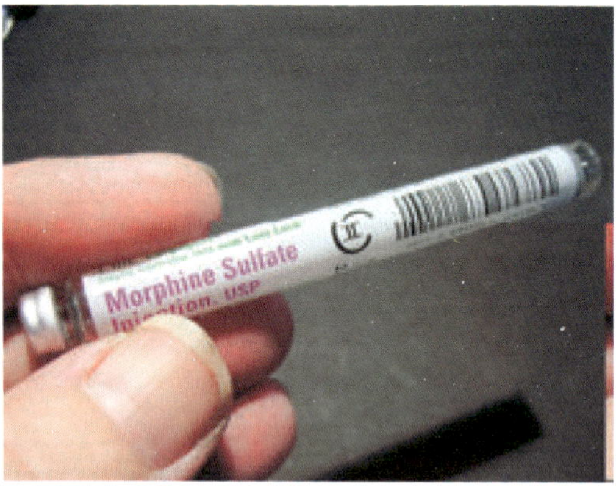

Morphine Injectable

MORPHINE

Trade Names

MS Contin
Avinza
Roxanol
Duramorph

Visual Description

Tablets, Pink Liquid

Methods of Use

Ingested, Injected, Snorted

Duration of Effects

Onset: Rapid w/injection; 15–60 minutes oral
Peak: 50–90 minutes; 15–60 minutes injected
Impaired: 3–6 Hours

Primary Symptoms of Use

Nystagmus: No
Lack of Convergence: No
Pulse: Below Normal
Pupils: Constricted
Pupillary Reaction To Light: Slow
Blood Pressure: Below Normal
Body Temperature: Normal/Below Normal

Other Symptoms

Depressed reflexes
Droopy eyelids (Ptosis)
Drowsiness
Dry mouth
Euphoria
Fresh puncture marks
Impaired divided attention
Low, raspy voice
Nausea
Poor motor coordination
Profuse scratching
Vomiting

Overdose Symptoms

Cold, clammy skin
Convulsions
Rapid, weak pulse
Slow, shallow breathing
Coma
Death

Additional Comments

Tolerance to narcotics develops quickly making drug dependence very likely.

OPIUM

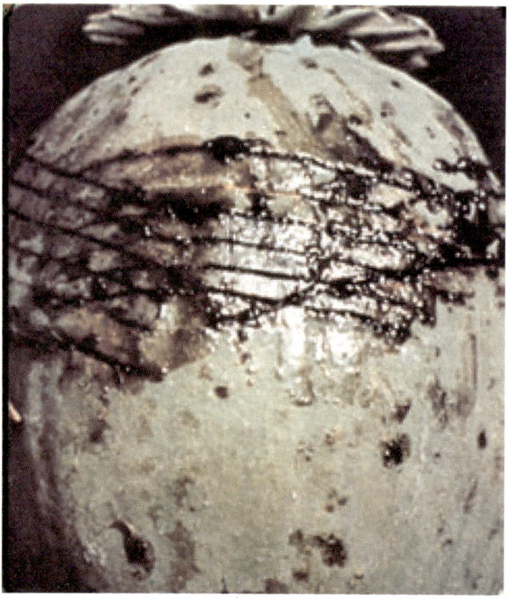

Opium poppy showing cuts to extract the raw opium.

OPIUM

Visual Description

Dark Brown Chunks, Powder

Methods of Use

Injected, Ingested (liquid, tea), Smoked, Snorted

Duration of Effects

Impaired: 4–6 Hours

Primary Symptoms of Use

Nystagmus: No
Lack of Convergence: No
Pulse: Below Normal
Pupils: Constricted
Pupillary Reaction To Light: Slow
Blood Pressure: Below Normal
Body Temperature: Normal/Below Normal

Other Symptoms

Depressed reflexes
Droopy eyelids (Ptosis)
Drowsiness
Dry mouth
Euphoria
Fresh puncture marks
Impaired divided attention
Low, raspy voice
Nausea
Poor motor coordination
Profuse scratching
Vomiting

Overdose Symptoms

Apnea
Cold, clammy skin
Convulsions
Delirium
Pulmonary edema
Rapid, weak pulse
Slow, shallow breathing
Coma
Death

Additional Comments

Tolerance to narcotics develops quickly making drug dependence very likely.

OXYCODONE

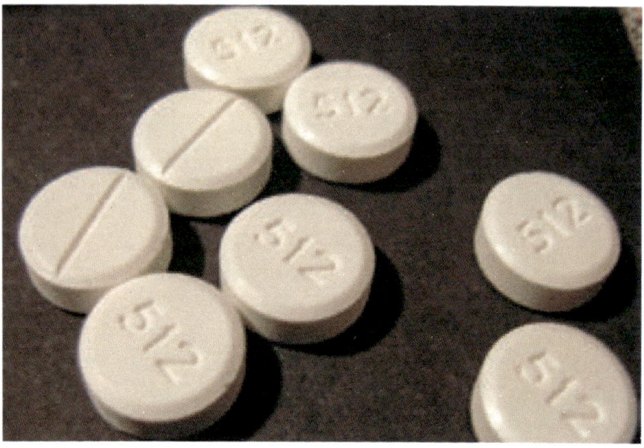

Percocet

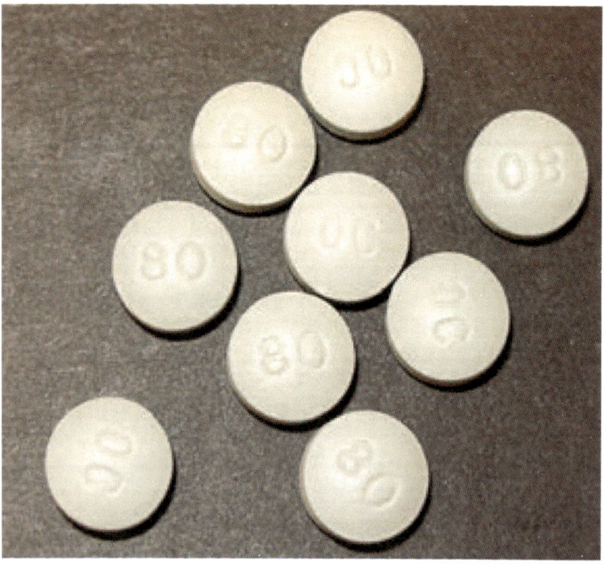

OxyContin 80mg

OXYCODONE

Common Trade Names & Combinations

Oxycodone—OxyContin, Oxydose, OxyFast, Tylox
Oxycodone & Acetaminophen—Percocet, Roxicet, Endocet, Oxycocet (Canadian)
Oxycodone & Aspirin—Percodan, Endodan, Oxycodan (Canadian)

Visual Description

Tablets, Drops, Liquid

Methods of Use

Ingested, Injected, Snorted, Smoked, Rectally

Duration of Effects

Onset: 15–30 minutes (oral)
Impaired: 4–6 Hours

Primary Symptoms of Use

Nystagmus: No
Lack of Convergence: No
Pulse: Below Normal
Pupils: Constricted
Pupillary Reaction To Light: Slow
Blood Pressure: Below Normal
Body Temperature: Normal/Below Normal

Other Symptoms

Depressed reflexes
Droopy eyelids (Ptosis)
Drowsiness
Dry mouth
Euphoria
Fresh puncture marks
Impaired divided attention
Low, raspy voice
Nausea
Poor motor coordination
Profuse scratching
Vomiting

Overdose Symptoms

Cold, clammy skin
Convulsions
Rapid, weak pulse
Slow, shallow breathing
Coma
Death

Additional Comments

Oxycontin was a popular brand of opiate to abuse. The makers of Oxycontin recently reformulated Oxycontin into a new form that is harder to abuse. Although some addicts have reported success with converting the new formula into an injectable form, addicts have moved on to other forms of Oxycodone.

ADDITIONAL NARCOTICS

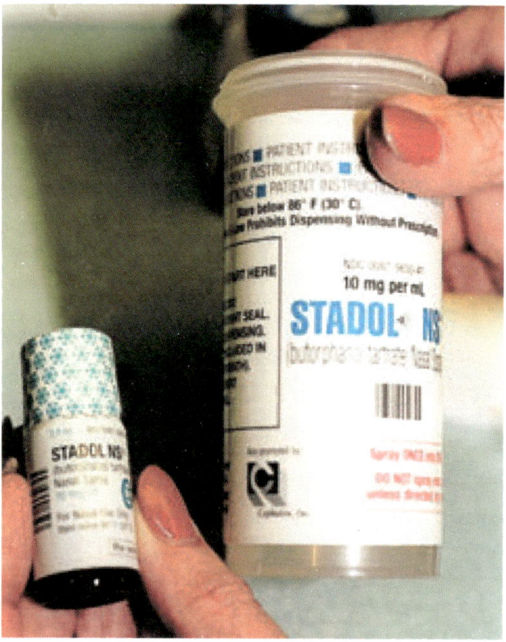

Butorphanol Tartrate - Stadol

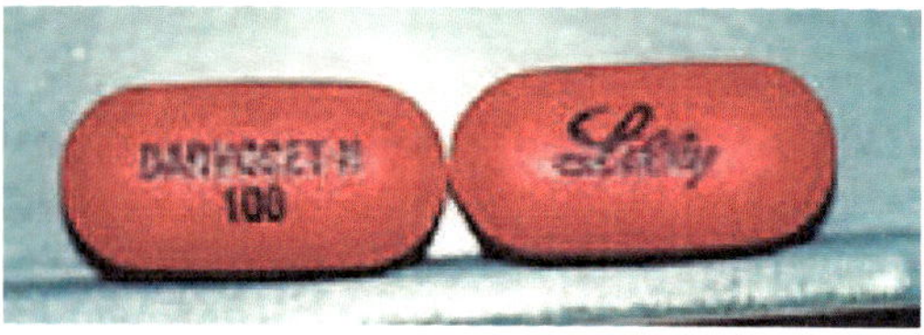

Propoxyphene & Acetaminophen - Darvocet

ADDITIONAL NARCOTICS

Trade names (representative)

Buprenorphine—Buprenex, Subutex (7–24 hours duration)
Butorphanol Tartrate—Stadol (nasal spray) (3–6 hours duration)
Propoxyphene & Acetaminophen—Darvocet (4–6 hours duration)
Propoxyphene—Darvon, Darvon—N (4–6 hours duration)
Nalbuphine—Nubain (3–6 hours duration)
Pentazocine—Talwin, Talacen, Talwin NX (2–3 hours duration)
Tramadol—Ultram (6–8 hours duration)

Additional Comments

Effects generally similar to other narcotic analgesics

BUPRENORPHINE

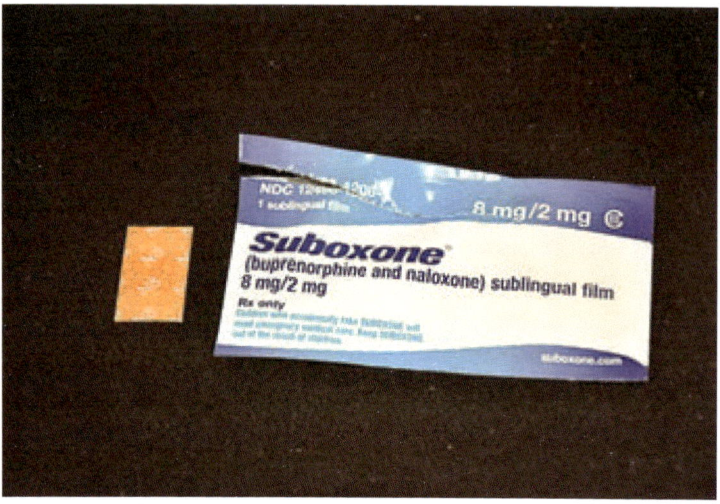

Suboxone, a trade-name of buprenorphine

BUPRENORPHINE

Common Trade Names

Subutex,
Suboxone
Zubsolv
Buprenex
Temgesic
Norspan
Butrans

Visual Description

Tablets
Sublingual film
Transdermal preparation
Solution for injection

Methods Of Use

Orally
Rectally (commonly referred to as "booty bumping" or "plugging"
Snorting

Duration of Effects

Onset: 15–30 minutes
Impaired: 4–6 hours

Possible Effects:

Nystagmus: No
Lack of Convergence: No
Pulse: Below Normal
Pupils: Constricted
Pupillary Reaction to Light: Slow
Blood Pressure: Below Normal
Body Temperature: Normal/Below Normal

Other Symptoms

Depressed reflexes
Droopy eyelids (Ptosis)
Drowsiness
Dry mouth
Euphoria
Fresh puncture marks
Impaired divided attention
Low, raspy voice
Nausea
Poor motor coordination
Profuse scratching
Vomiting

Overdose Symptoms

Cold, clammy skin
Convulsions
Rapid, weak pulse
Slow, shallow breathing
Coma
Death

Additional Comments

Buprenorphine is often prescribed to people who are addicted to opiates. One ingredient in some formulations is naloxone (sometimes referred to as Narcan). This is an opiate antagonist, or an opioid blocker. In order to get high, users will crush suboxone pills prescribed for their addiction and then snort it, which by-passes the opiate antagonist properties.

KRATOM

Botanical Name: Mitragyna speciosa

Kratom Tree

Dried Kratom leaves about to be brewed into a euphoric tea.

25 Size 0 capsules of 500mg of Kratom. It takes approximately 10 caps to induce an opiate-like euphoria.

KRATOM

Botanical Name: Mitragyna speciosa

Visual Description

Source is a tropical tree primarily in South East Asia, up to 50 feet tall; same family as coffee tree. Distributed as leaves (whole or crushed), powder, extract, resin extract "pies" or pellets. Seeds also seen available on Internet

Methods of Use

Leaf is chewed for stimulant effect or brewed into tea. May also be boiled & mixed with cola or cough syrup. Some reports of "juice" preparation. Described as having a combination of stimulant and opiate effects, usually varying with dosage.

Duration of Effects

Onset: within 10 minutes, reportedly fading within several hours

Primary Symptoms of Use

- Low doses may produce primarily stimulant effects
  - Increased alertness
  - Talkativeness
  - Increased physical activity
- Higher doses produce opiate effects
  - Reduced pain response
  - Sedation
  - Mild euphoria
- Addiction may result from chronic use
- Psychoactive effects may result especially with chronic use
  - Hallucinations
  - Confusion
- Constipation
- Nausea

Street Names

Thang, Kakuam, Thom, Ketum

Additional Comments

Kratom is unscheduled in the U.S. at this time. Knowledge of this drug is somewhat limited. Some have reported using it to mitigate the withdrawal from opiates. It is an unusual drug with varying effects. We are including it in the NARCOTICS section at this time due to its primary effects being most comparable to opiates.

This page intentionally left blank.

DISSOCIATIVE ANESTHETICS

PCP
Phencyclidine

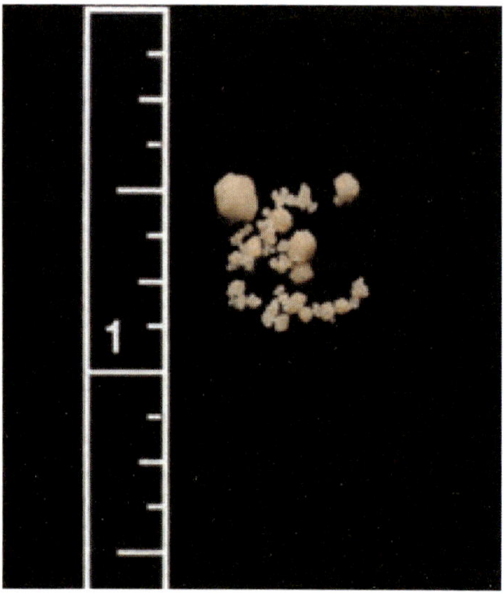

Powdered PCP

PCP in Liquid Form

PCP
Phencyclidine

Visual Description
White or brown powder, pills, capsules, light to medium gold liquid. Occasionally found mixed with meth in pills sold as Ecstasy

Methods of Use
Ingested; smoked (marijuana or tobacco cigarette dipped in PCP); absorbed; inhaled; injected.

Duration of Effects
Onset: 1–5 Minutes
Loaded: 4–6 Hours
Peak: 15–30 Minutes
Overdose Symptoms: 24 Hrs or Longer

Primary Symptoms of Use
Nystagmus: Yes
Lack of Convergence: Yes
Pulse: Elevated
Pupils: Near Normal
Pupillary Reaction To Light: Near Normal
Blood Pressure: Elevated
Body Temperature: Elevated (PCP users may strip off their clothes to cool off)

Other Symptoms:
Agitation & aggression
Analgesia (pain block, high pain threshold)
Catatonia
Cyclic behavior
Disoriented
Dysphoria
Emergence delirium
Eyelid tremors
Fascination w/water
Fearful
Long, intense trips
Muscle rigidity
Non-communicative
Odor of substance
Paranoia
Perspiring
Repetitive speech
Synesthesia
Warm to the touch

Overdose Symptoms
Bizarre behavior
Long, intense trips
Psychosis
Violence
Death

Additional Comments
"Embalming fluid" is an old nickname for PCP. Formaldehyde (embalming fluid ingredient) was often added to slow the burn. More recently, some have abused so-called wet, fry, or illy sticks which are marijuana cigarettes dipped in either pure PCP, the combination, or pure formaldehyde (produces bizarre behavior but not the pain blocking effect of PCP). Avoid loud noises, bright lights or sudden movements with subjects under the influence.

KETAMINE
(Special K)

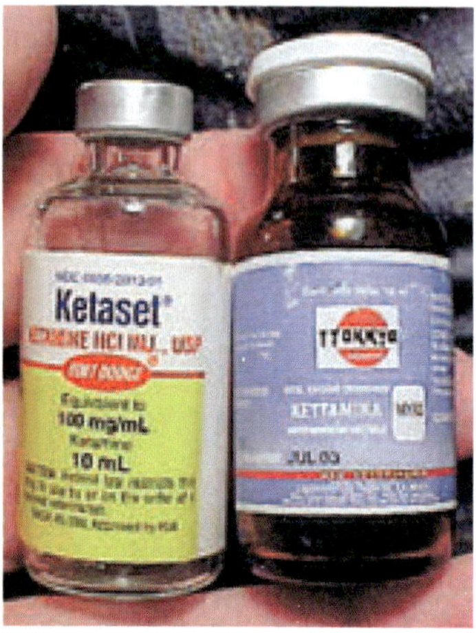

Legitimate (left) and counterfeit (right) Ketamine vials

Ketamine vial and powder

KETAMINE
(Special K)

Visual Description
Clear liquid (very light amber color) often in injectable-type vial; white powder.

Methods of Use
Ingested; snorted; smoked; injected; rectal insertion.

Duration of Effects
Onset: Rapid
Pain Block: 30 minutes to 2 hours (dose dependent)
Amnesia effect up to 2 hours

Primary Symptoms of Use
Nystagmus: Yes
Lack of Convergence: Yes
Pulse: Elevated
Pupils: Near Normal
Pupillary Reaction To Light: Near Normal
Blood Pressure: Elevated
Body Temperature: Elevated

Other Symptoms:
Analgesia (pain block)
Apnea
Catatonic state (The K-Hole)
Delirium
Emergence delirium (bizarre or violent behavior)
Flashbacks
Hallucinations (vivid)
Insomnia
Seizures
Tremors
Vomiting
Coma
Cardiac arrest

Additional Comments
Avoid stimulation such as loud noises and rapid movements around subjects under the influence to reduce emergence delirium. May have flashbacks.

DEXTROMETHORPHAN
(DXM)
Cough Suppressant

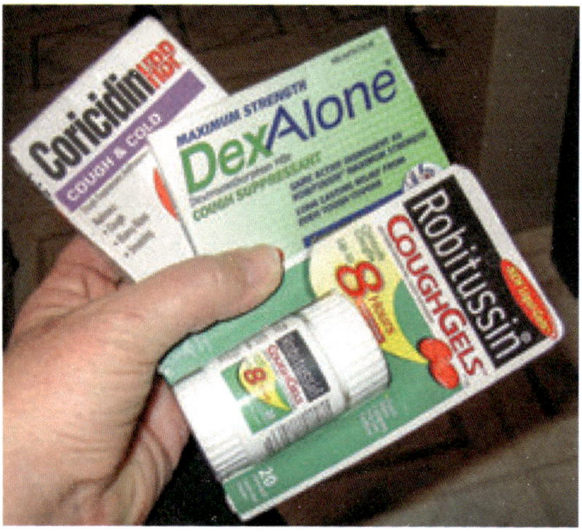

Common commercial DXM products

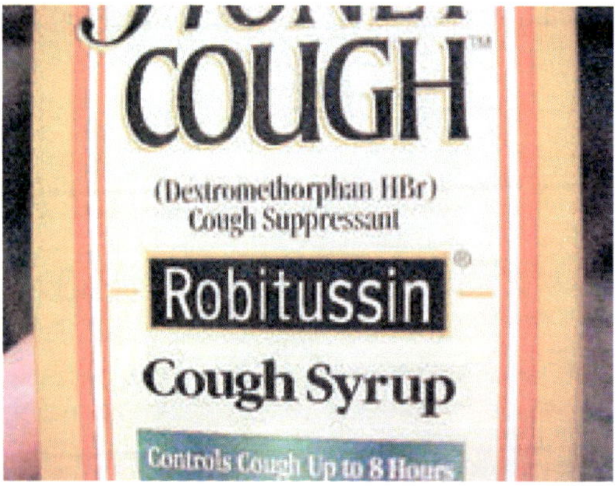

Common liquid DXM product

DXM – Street name "Triple C" tablets

DEXTROMETHORPHAN
(DXM)
Cough Suppressant

DXM is a common ingredient as a cough suppressant in numerous over-the-counter products and is not a controlled substance at this time. It is a highly abused substance nationwide, especially among young teens because of its legal availability. Even teens with money to buy the product sometimes shoplift because this act is virtually part of the culture of the DXM crowd. Normal dosing involves one or two pills or doses of cough syrup every four hours. Abusers may take 10 to 45 pills at a time or fairly rapid succession as they seek to achieve the various "plateaus" of experiences described on Internet websites such as www.dextroverse.org and www.erowid.org, two of many pro-drug websites. Some rank DXM with depressants but in higher doses, it is closer in effects to PCP and ketamine, making it an atypical dissociative anesthetic or narcotic analgesic. The effects are also complicated by the fact that it is often taken in pills with other ingredients as well, causing variations on effect. Websites instruct abusers on extracting DXM from cough syrups and pills that contain other medications to avoid the interactions and high doses of the other ingredients.

Duration

Onset: 15–30 minutes (oral), more rapid if snorted
Duration 6 hours

Visual Description

Gel capsule, pill or liquid, varying with product, and may be seen in powder form.

Primary Symptoms of Use:

Nystagmus: Yes
Lack of Convergence: Yes
Pulse: Elevated
Pupils: Near Normal (May be dilated with DXM)
Pupillary Reaction To Light: Near Normal
Blood Pressure: Elevated
Body Temperature: Elevated

Other Symptoms:

Ataxia
Coma
Excitation
Fever
Hyperactivity, and in high doses dissociative effects similar to PCP or ketamine
Hypertension
Hyperthermia
Insomnia
Respiratory depression
Tremors

Terms & Products

Robotripping, Robitussin DM, Coricidin Cough & Cold (AKA: CCC, Triple C), The Matrix (for the red CCC pills), Skittles and Skittling, DexAlone, Simply Cough, Vicks 44 Cough Relief, Benylin, Creomulsion Cough, ElixSure, Silphen DMetc. Any product containing DXM is a potential target for abuse. DexAlone contains no other ingredients.

This page intentionally left blank.

STIMULANTS

AMPHETAMINES

Amphetamine & Dextroamphetamine (Adderal)l 10 mg

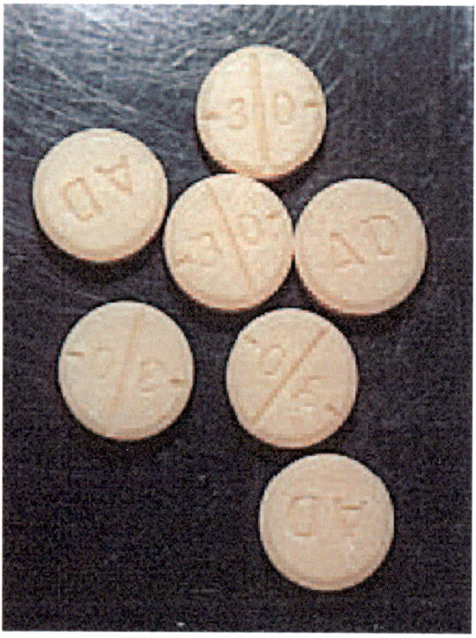

Amphetamine & Dextroamphetamine (Adderall) 30 mg

AMPHETAMINES

Drug Name—Representative Tradename

Amphetamine and Dextroamphetamine—Adderall
Dextroamphetamine—Dexedrine, Dextrostat (Canada)
Methylphenidate—Ritalin, Concerta, Metadate, Riphenidate (Canada)
Pemoline—Cylert (no longer marketed in the U.S.)
Methamphetamine—Desoxyn

Visual Description

Various shapes/colors/doses of capsules or pills, depending on brand and dosage. May also be found in powder.

Methods of Use

These are prescription drugs typically used for treatment of attention deficit disorders, narcolepsy or exogenous obesity. But they have become widely diverted as stay-awake pills for students, working adults, etc. Abusers may take them as pills or crush them into powder for snorting or even convert to liquid for injecting.

Duration of Effects

Onset: 30 seconds (snorted/injected) to 1½ hours (oral)
Duration: 4–8 hours (Concerta is a slow-release version of Ritalin)

Primary Symptoms of Use

Nystagmus: No
Lack of Convergence: No
Pulse: Elevated
Pupils: Dilated (Long term users may have constricted pupils)
Pupillary Reaction To Light: Slow
Blood Pressure: Elevated
Body Temperature: Elevated

Other Symptoms

Anxiety
Arrhythmia
Body tremors
Decreased appetite
Dizziness
Dry mouth
Euphoria
Excitation
Grinding teeth (bruxism)
Hallucinations
Headaches
Hypertension
Impaired divided attention
Increased alertness
Insomnia
Psychomotor agitation or retardation
Restlessness
Sexual impairment
Sweating
Weight loss

Overdose Symptoms

Coma
Convulsions
Death
Seizures
Vomiting

Additional Comments

High levels of amphetamines or injected doses can create a sudden rise in blood pressure that can cause a stroke, very high fever or heart attack. Prolonged use can cause hallucination, delusions and paranoia. Even chewing tablets versus swallowing can increase side effects and decrease efficacy for those using legitimately. Pemoline dropped due to increased liver function risks.

COCAINE
(Crack or Freebase)

Cocaine: Crack or Freebase

Cocaine: 18th Street Style

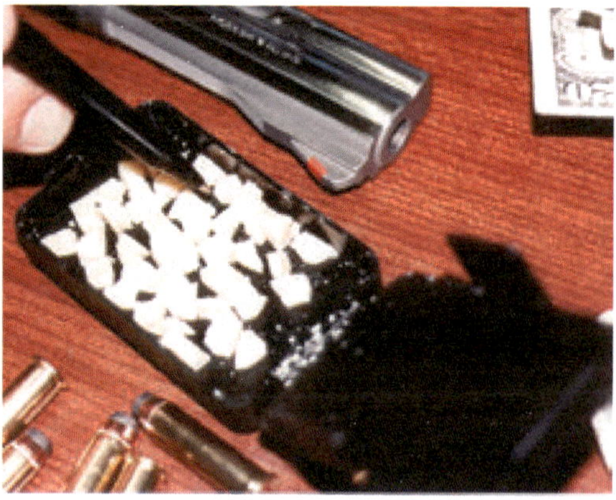

Cocaine: Dope, Money and the Gun

COCAINE
(Crack or Freebase)

Visual Description

Light brown, beige or white crystalline rocks often packaged in small vials or zip-lock plastic bags. May also be found in "cookie" shapes when made in the bottom of small containers and not yet broken/cut into pieces. Though most often made with baking soda, coke powder may also be converted with baking soda, flour, yeast and carbonated beverage, resulting in a more bubbled texture.

Methods of Use

Smoked

Duration of Effects

Onset: 8–30 seconds Duration: 10–20 minutes
Peak: 5 minutes

Primary Symptoms of Use

Nystagmus: No
Lack of Convergence: No
Pulse: Elevated
Pupils: Dilated (Long term users may have constricted pupils)
Pupillary Reaction To Light: Slow
Blood Pressure: Elevated
Body Temperature: Elevated

Other Symptoms

Anxiety
Apnea
Ataxia
Body tremors
Decreased appetite
Dental erosion (chronic use)
Depression
Dizziness
Dry mouth
Euphoria
Excitation
Fresh puncture marks
Grinding teeth (bruxism)
Hallucinations
Headaches
Hypertension
Impaired divided attention
Impotence
Increased alertness
Insomnia
Paranoia
Restlessness
Running/red/bleeding nose
Seizures
Sweating
Talkative
Weight loss

Overdose Symptoms

Agitation, extreme
Coma
Convulsions
Death

Additional Comments

Traditional rock cocaine somewhat resembles pieces of macadamia nut, though harder in texture. Freebasing cocaine using ether is a less common and much more dangerous method (severe burns can result if smoked before the ether has completely evaporated). Waxy or soapy in appearance.

COCAINE

Cocaine Powder

Powdered cocaine is placed on a mirror or piece of glass or other flat, non-porous surface. It is then chopped into a fine powder with a razor blade or credit card. The cocaine is then spread into thin lines, and the lines are then snorted through a tube, drinking straw or rolled currency. See **"Snorting Cocaine" on page 147**.

Kilo packages ("Kilos") of Cocaine

COCAINE

Visual Description

White crystalline (shiny) powder (may be "cut" or diluted with other products such as procaine, lidocaine, mannitol, ephedrine, sucrose, lactose, tetracaine, benzocaine, etc., to extend the quantity of product). Has surfaced as "black" cocaine to attempt to fool law enforcement, using charcoal, cobalt, iron dust, etc., to alter the color. May be found in bindles, plastic baggies, or pressed into kilos. Markings on kilos may indicate the producer or the intended recipient.

Methods of Use

Snorted, injected. (Chewing coca leaf provides a mild stimulant effect).

Duration of Effects

Onset

Injected: immediate Snorted: 2–3 minutes
Oral: within 1 hour

Loaded: 5–45 minutes Oral ingestion: 1–2 hours
Peak: 5–15 minutes

Primary Symptoms of Use

Nystagmus: No
Lack of Convergence: No
Pulse: Elevated
Pupils: Dilated (Long term users may have constricted pupils)
Pupillary Reaction To Light: Slow
Blood Pressure: Elevated
Body Temperature: Elevated

Other Symptoms

Anxiety
Apnea
Ataxia
Body tremors
Decreased appetite
Dental erosion (chronic use)
Depression
Dizziness
Dry mouth
Euphoria
Excitation
Fresh puncture marks
Grinding teeth (bruxism)
Hallucinations
Headaches
Hypertension
Impaired divided attention
Impotence
Increased alertness
Insomnia
Paranoia
Restlessness
Running/stuffy/red/bleeding nose
Seizures
Sweating
Talkative
Weight loss

Overdose Symptoms

Agitation, extreme
Convulsions
Coma
Death

Additional Comments

Long-term use may result in ulceration of the mucous membranes of the nose or complete perforation of the nasal septum. Schedule II because it does have limited legitimate use as a topical anesthesia of the mucous membranes for medical procedures.

METHAMPHETAMINE
(Crank or Speed)

Methamphetamine

Methamphetamine

METHAMPHETAMINE
(Crank or Speed)

Visual Description
Powder or chunks of various shades from white to beige, orange or pink (dye from type of source pills used for ephedrine or pseudoephedrine). Like cocaine, it may be adulterated with "cuts" to extend the quantity or to clean up the color; common cut is a dietary supplement MSM (methyl-sulfonyl methane). Also marketed in prescription tablet as Desoxyn for short-term weight loss and attention deficit disorder.

"Ice" or crystal meth: white crystalline rock; freebase form of methamphetamine, typically of high purity. May look like chunks of ice or shards of glass.

Methods of Use
Injected, smoked, snorted, swallowed

Duration of Effects
Onset: 5–20 minutes (snorted) 30–60 minutes (oral) within seconds (smoked)
Duration: 6–18 hours

Primary Symptoms of Use
Nystagmus: No
Lack of Convergence: No
Pulse: Elevated
Pupils: Dilated (Long term users may have constricted pupils)
Pupillary Reaction To Light: Slow
Blood Pressure: Elevated
Body Temperature: Elevated

Other Symptoms
Anxiety
Body tremors
Decreased appetite
Dizziness
Dry mouth
Euphoria
Excitation
Grinding teeth (bruxism)
Hallucinations
Impaired divided attention
Increased alertness
Insomnia
Loss of coordination
Paranoia
Puncture marks
Restlessness
Sexual stimulation
Sweating
Weight loss

Overdose Symptoms
Agitation
Coma
Convulsions
Death
Hallucinations
Psychosis

Additional Comments
Large meth labs may involve extensive chemical lists and laboratory equipment; small labs may involve only easily obtained ingredients and homemade conversion of common items. "Ice" is crystal meth, a smokable form of methamphetamine. Use first started in the Far East, then Hawaii, with use/manufacturing based in South Korea, the Philippines, Honk Kong and Japan. Now found in a much more widespread pattern in the United States.

METHCATHINONE

N-Methyl-Cathinone (AKA: "Cat")

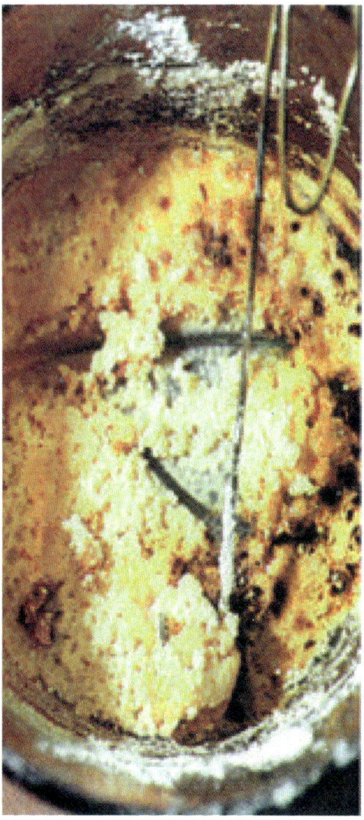

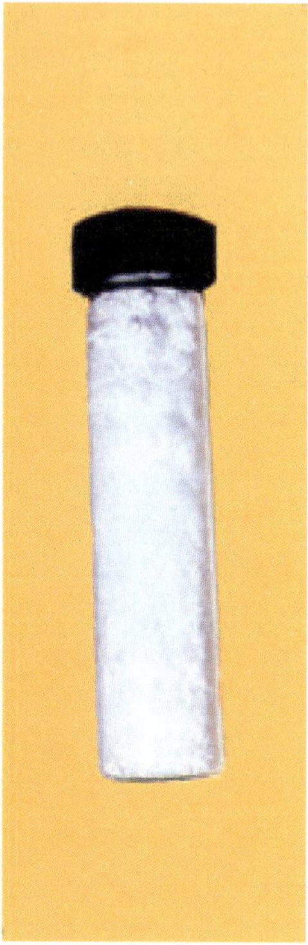

METHCATHINONE

N-Methyl-Cathinone (AKA: "Cat")

Visual Description
Off-white, light yellow or beige powder

Methods of Use
Injected, snorted, smoked or taken orally

Duration of Effects
Loaded: from 30 minutes to 24 hours depending on dosage

Primary Symptoms of Use
Nystagmus: No
Lack of Convergence: No
Pulse: Elevated
Pupils: Dilated (Long term users may have constricted pupils)
Pupillary Reaction To Light: Slow
Blood Pressure: Elevated
Body Temperature: Elevated

Other Symptoms
Anxiety
Impaired divided attention
Body tremors
Increased alertness
Decreased appetite
Insomnia
Dizziness
Loss of coordination
Euphoria
Paranoia
Excitation
Puncture marks
Grinding teeth (bruxism)
Restlessness
Hallucinations

Overdose Symptoms
Agitation
Coma
Convulsions
Death
Fever
Hallucinations
Psychosis

Additional Comments
Though easily made and similar to methamphetamine, this drug has been mostly centered in the Midwest and not widely favored. Just as with methamphetamine, ephedrine or pseudoephedrine is the key ingredient. Norephedrine (phenylpropanolamine) can be substituted, resulting in cathinone rather than methcathinone (see Cathinone, page 126).

In early 2009 a drug believed to be 4-methylmethcathinone (4-MMC) (AKA: "Sunshine") surfaced in Oregon. This drug had been reported earlier in Australia, Sweden and Denmark. Though related chemically to methcathinone, the effects of methylmethcathinone are supposedly akin to crystal meth plus some of the psychotropic effects of MDMA (Ecstasy) and other phenethylamines.

4-METHYLMETHCATHINONE
(Mephedrone, Meow, M-cat)

Mephedrone

4-METHYLMETHCATHINONE

(Mephedrone, Meow, M-cat)

Visual description

White powder, can be put into capsules

Methods of use

Orally, snorting, injection, rectally (booty bumping, plugging)

Primary Symptoms of Use

Nystagmus: No
Lack of Convergence: No
Pulse: Elevated
Pupils: Dilated (Long term users may have constricted pupils)
Pupillary Reaction To Light: Slow
Blood Pressure: Elevated
Body Temperature: Elevated

Other Symptoms

Anxiety
Impaired divided attention
Body tremors
Increased alertness
Decreased appetite
Insomnia
Dizziness
Loss of coordination
Euphoria
Paranoia
Excitation
Puncture marks
Grinding teeth (bruxism)
Restlessness
Hallucinations

Overdose Symptoms

Agitation
Coma
Convulsions
Death
Fever
Hallucinations
Psychosis

Additional Comments

Mephedrone is one of hundreds of designer drugs or legal highs that have been reported in recent years, including artificial chemicals such as synthetic cannabis and semisynthetic substances such as methylhexanamine. These drugs are primarily developed to avoid being controlled by laws against illegal drugs, thus giving them the label of designer drugs.

CATHINONE

AKA: Khat—Catha Edulis plant
(Pronounced "Cot")

Khat - Rolled and tied for distribution

CATHINONE

AKA: Khat—Catha Edulis plant

(Pronounced "Cot")

Visual Description

White powder if synthesized (similar to making methamphetamine or methcathinone). Or, plant material from a flowering evergreen tree or large shrub. Leaves are described as green to crimson-brown and glossy, but may become yellow-green and leathery as they age/dry.

Methods of Use

Chewing the leaves, drinking plant juice

Duration of Effects

Onset: 20 minutes
Duration: 2 hours

Primary Symptoms of Use

Nystagmus: No
Lack of Convergence: No
Pulse: Elevated
Pupils: Dilated (Long term users may have constricted pupils)
Pupillary Reaction To Light: Slow
Blood Pressure: Elevated
Body Temperature: Elevated

Other Symptoms

Anesthetic properties
Anxiety
Body tremors
Decreased appetite
Dizziness
Euphoria
Excitation
Impaired divided attention
Increased alertness
Insomnia
Paranoia
Restlessness

Overdose Symptoms

Breathing difficulties
Coma
Convulsions
Death
Psychosis

Additional Comments

Plant comes primarily from Eastern Africa at high altitudes. Khat contains cathinone when leaves are fresh. As leaves dry (unrefrigerated more than 48 hours), contents deteriorate to contain only cathine, a lesser stimulant.

MDPV (METHYLENEDIOXYPRYROVALERONE)

(AKA: Bath Salts)

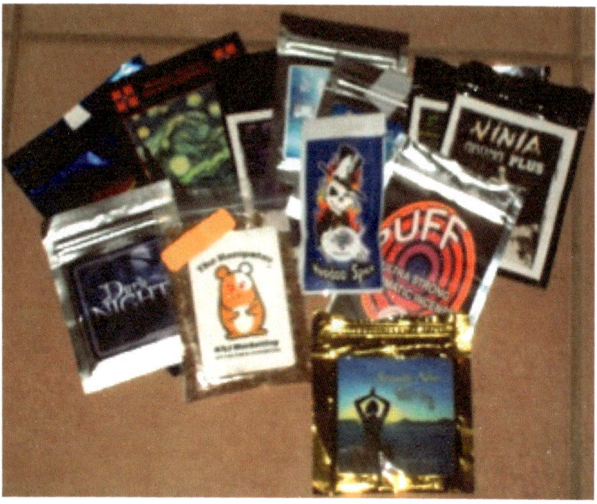

Bath Salts

Bath Salts

MDPV (METHYLENEDIOXYPRYROVALERONE)

(AKA: Bath Salts)

Visual Description

The substance appears as a pure white to light-brown, clumpy powder with a slight odor. It appears to darken slightly in color and take on a potato-like odor if exposed to air for any significant length of time. It has also been observed to rapidly degrade and change properties when in exposed to air as a free base.

Methods of Use

Snorted, injected, smoked, mixed with food, mixed with drinks,

Duration of Effects

For snorting:

Onset: 5–20 minutes
Coming up: 15–30 minutes
Plateau: 30–120 minutes
Coming down: 30–60 minutes
After affects: 2–48 hours

Primary Symptoms of Use

Nystagmus: No
Lack of Convergence: No
Pulse: Elevated
Pupils: Dilated (Long term users may have constricted pupils)
Pupillary Reaction To Light: Slow
Blood Pressure: Elevated
Body Temperature: Elevated

Other Symptoms

Anesthetic properties
Anxiety
Body tremors
Decreased appetite
Dizziness
Euphoria
Excitation
Impaired divided attention
Increased alertness
Insomnia
Paranoia
Restlessness

Overdose Symptoms

Breathing difficulties
Coma
Convulsions
Death
Psychosis

Additional Comments

MDPV had been previously unregulated because they aren't marketed or intended for human consumption. It is marketed in the U.S. as "Bath Salts" and is found in convenience stores, discount tobacco outlets, gas stations, pawnshops, tattoo parlors, truck stops, night clubs and other locations. The marketing scheme is similar to that for Spice, K2 which was sold as incense, and herbal smoking blends.

ADDITIONAL STIMULANTS

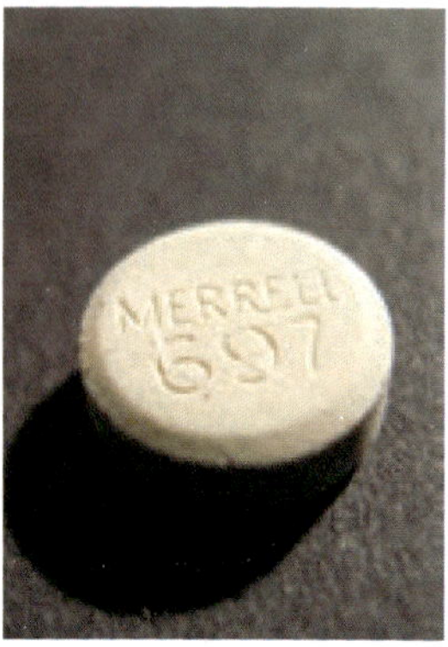

Diethylpropion Tenuate

(Photo courtesy of Christine Larson, AZDPS)

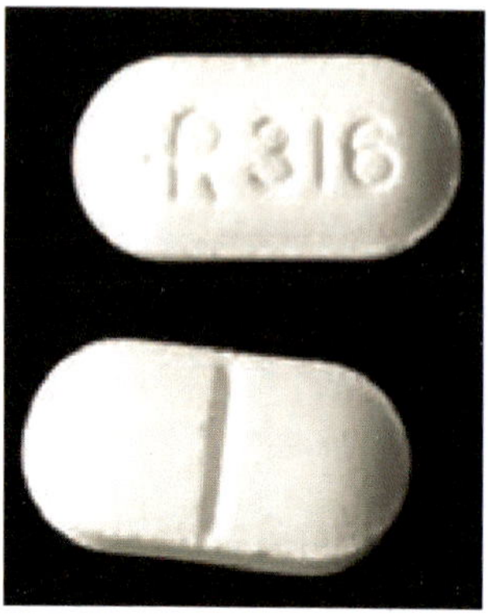

Phentermine

(Photo courtesy of Christine Larson, AZDPS)

Drinks Containing Taurine

Caplet contains 12mg ephedrine group alkaloids

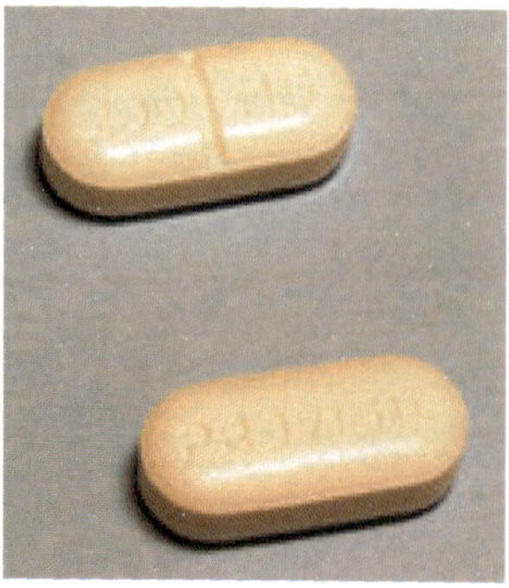

Provigil 200 mg

ADDITIONAL STIMULANTS

Drug Name—Representative Tradename

Diethylpropion—Tenuate, Dospan (anorectic—for weight loss, stimulant effects)
Mazindol—Mazanor, Sanorex (anorectic for weight loss and narcolepsy)
Phenmetrazine—Nistenal, Preludin (anorectic)
Phendimetrazine—Prelu-2 (anorectic)
Benzphetamine—Didrex (anorectic)
Phentermine—Adipex, Fastin, Ionamin (anorectic)
Fenfluramine or **Dexfenfluramine—**Pondimin, Redux

Visual Description

Various pills, capsules or powder

Methods of Use

Taken as pills or snorted

Duration of Effects

Similar to other stimulants, varying with product

Primary Symptoms of Use

Similar to other stimulants

Additional Comments

Fen Phen, a once popular diet pill combination, was a combination of phentermine and fenfluramine or dexfenfluramine that was linked to excessive cases of primary pulmonary hypertension, resulting in numerous lawsuits.

OTHER CHEMICALS WITH STIMULANT PROPERTIES

Ephedrine & Pseudoephedrine (also Ma Huang)
Bitter Orange—citrus aurantium (synephrine)
Kola nut extract
Taurine (featured in large quantity in numerous energy drinks)
Caffeine (also called Guarana)
Yohimbe

Additional Comments

These chemicals may cause typical stimulant properties such as increased heart rate, increased body temperature, etc., and may be encountered in DUI or overdose cases. Bitter orange, kola nut, taurine and caffeine are often included in supplements in very large quantities as ephedrine alternatives or in addition to ephedrine, but may harbor some of the same risk factors as taking ephedrine. Relatively little research has been done re ongoing ingestion of large quantities of such ingredients.

Continued on the next page.

ADDITIONAL EMERGING STIMULANTS OF ABUSE

Modafinil—Provigil (daytime sleepiness, narcolepsy)

Modafinil is said to be relatively free of typical stimulant side effects such as agitation, irritability, nervousness, euphoria or the potential for paranoid delusion and addiction that are common to other stimulants (when used a directed). Modafinil targets very specific regions of the brain believed to regulate normal wakefulness. This drug is being touted for shift-work related sleepiness, daytime sleepiness and narcolepsy. While "abuse" may not follow traditional stimulant patterns, over use of it may result in fatigue after the fact and thus result in impaired driving. Effects may include blurred vision, dizziness, dry mouth, insomnia, depression, confusion, mood swings, nervousness, anxiety or agitation, etc.

Fenethylline—Captagon & Theophylline—Slo-Phyllin

Captagon is an internationally recognized trademark name for the drug fenethylline; it is no longer legally made and is not used in the U.S. under any trademark. Slo-Phyllin is a U.S. trademark name for the drug theophylline, which is used for respiratory diseases, such as asthma. Fenethylline metabolizes (breaks down) in the human body into amphetamine and theophylline (which is a lower level stimulant, somewhat similar to caffeine). Though no longer legally made, fenethylline is still commonly referred to as Captagon and is an increasingly popular drug of abuse in the Arab countries, particularly Saudi Arabia. Large seizures are becoming common in that region. Pills may resemble MDMA (Ecstasy) and may even be sold as Ecstasy. Contents may actually be illegally-made fenethylline or other mixtures merely being represented as fenethylline. Due to the international trafficking patterns of Ecstasy-type drugs and the increased contact of American troops, contractors and others with countries abusing fenethylline, there is a potential for growing exposure in the U.S. to fenethylline and a potential for increased abuse interest in the caffeine-level stimulant theophylline.

ANDROGENIC ANABOLIC STEROIDS

ANDROGENIC ANABOLIC STEROIDS

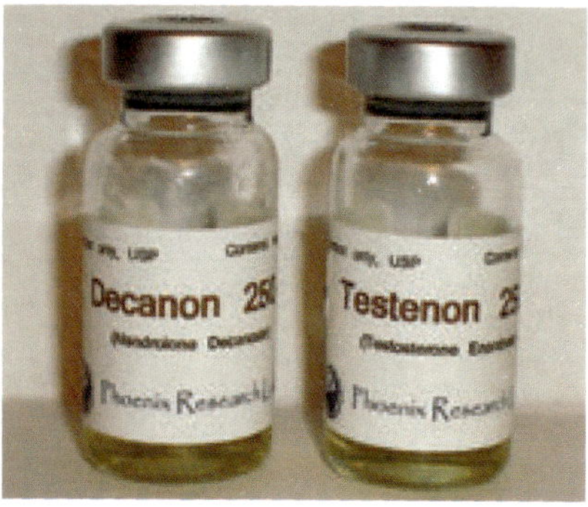

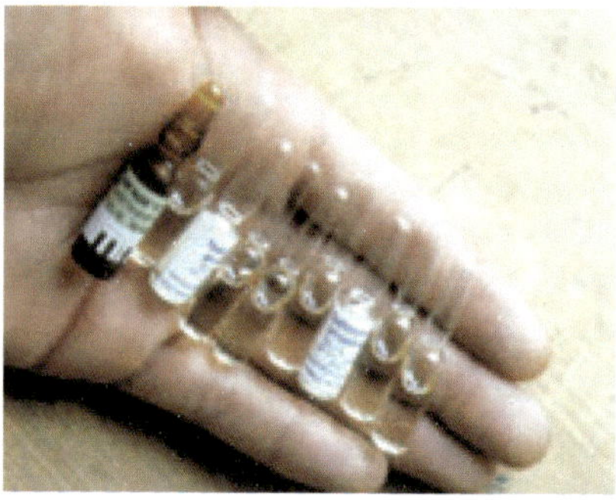

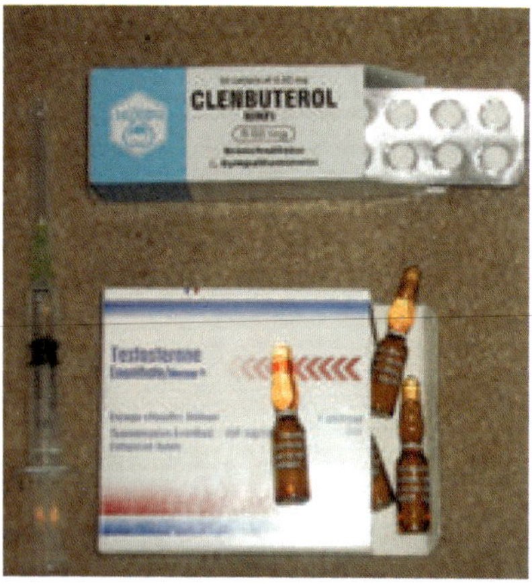

(Photo courtesy South Dakota Highway Patrol)

ANDROGENIC ANABOLIC STEROIDS

Street Names

Juice, roids, stackers, gym candy, pumpers, arnolds

Representative names

Anadrol—oxymetholone
Dianabol—methandrostenolone
Deca-Durabolin—nandrolone decanoate
Depo-Testosterone—testosterone cypionate
Durabolin—nandrolone phenpropionate
Equipose—veterinary product, boldenone undecylenate
Halotestin—fluxoymesterone
Oxandrin—oxandrolone
Winstrol—stanozolol

Visual Description

Various shapes and colors of pills, clear or yellow to gold colored liquid in glass vials, loaded syringes

Methods of Use

Taken orally or most commonly injected (often in unusual locations, trying to avoid areas visual when wearing swim trunks or bikini). Multiple doses of various anabolic steroids (stacking) is typically done to maximize effectiveness in case some of the product is fake and worthless. Typically taken for a specific period, followed by a period off of them and then resuming use (called "cycling"). Legitimate steroids also include gels or patches or implanted pellets. Abuse levels may be up to 100 times the therapeutic amounts.

Primary Symptoms of Use

Adverse cardiovascular effects
Cancer risks
Cholesterol changes
Fluid retention
High blood pressure
Increased aggression or bizarre behavior (known as "roid rage")
Infertility
Liver disorders (jaundice, liver damage)
Severe acne

Other Symptoms—Teens

Prematurely stunted skeletal growth
Rapid rate of puberty changes

Other Symptoms—Males

Atrophy of testicles
Reduced sperm production
Baldness
Development of breasts (gynecomastia, also called "bitch tits")
Increased chance of prostate enlargement and/or cancer

Continued on the next page.

Other Symptoms—Females

Enlarged clitoris
Facial hair growth
Male-pattern baldness
Masculinization of facial hair, depth of voice
Menstrual irregularity

Additional Comments

Legally used for body wasting diseases (patients with AIDS, for example) and those born with insufficient natural production of testosterone for normal development. Abused illegally by athletes (and some law enforcement officers & firefighters) for increased strength and size, by bodybuilders for dramatic body appearance and by teens for athletic performance, size (often to overcome being a victim of bullying) or appearance (females, for example, seeking a lean look by taking steroids but not doing intense workouts which would build bulk).

PARAPHERNALIA IDENTIFICATION AND DESCRIPTIONS

MARIJUANA SMOKING PARAPHERNALIA

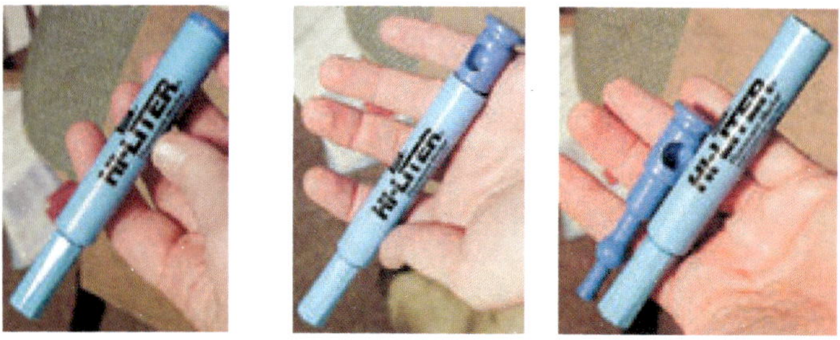

HI-LITER® Pipe

"Chapstick" Pipe

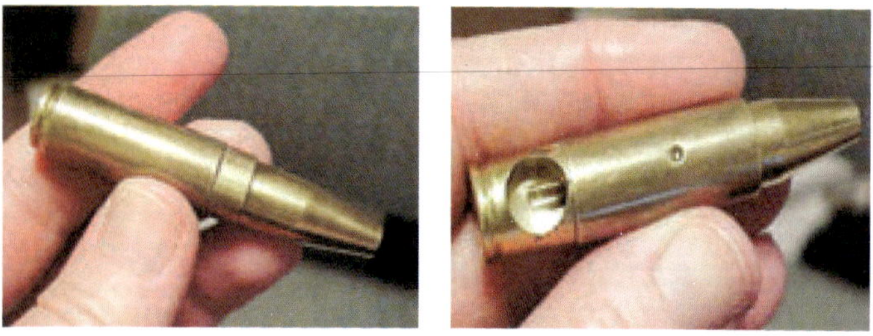

Bullet Pipe

MARIJUANA ROACH CLIPS

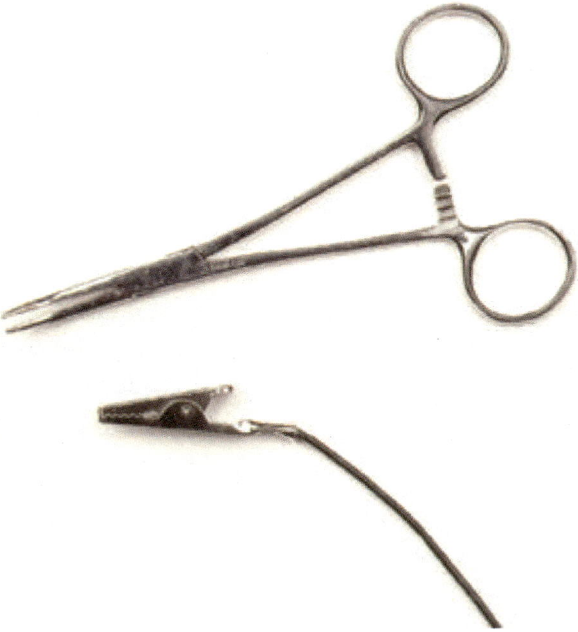

"Roach Clips" are used to hold the last bit of a burning marijuana cigarette. In addition to the devices shown, small tweezers may also be used.

OTHER TYPES OF SMOKING PARAPHERNALIA

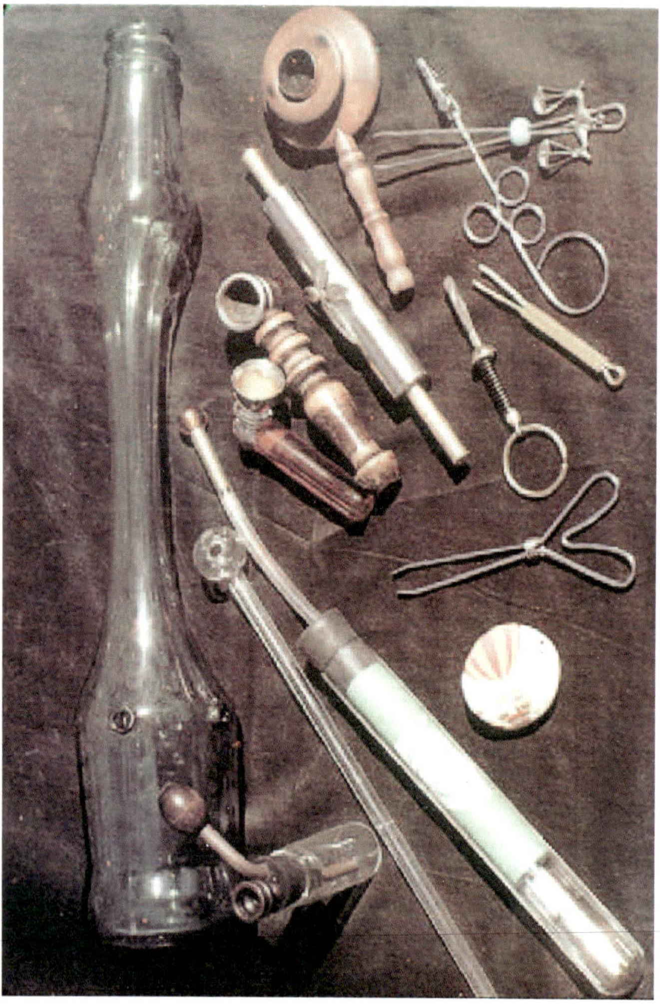

Assorted Crack, Hash, and Marijuana Smoking Paraphernalia

FREEBASE SMOKING PIPE

After placing a piece of copper scouring pad, steel wool or Brillo Pad in the bowl, the Freebase Rock is placed on top and lit. The rock will begin to vaporize and melt. Since the vapors are heavier than air, they drop into the neck of the pipe and are drawn into the lungs. Some pipes have a bulge or chamber in the neck of the pipe that is used to collect the vapor and allow it to accumulate before it is inhaled into the lungs. This chamber is also used for cooling the vapor. A glass or metal tube, called a "Straight Shooter" is also used. Often made from automotive radio antennas, they are readily obtained and can be easily dropped if authorities should approach.

See **Wash-Back Methods** on page 162

METHAMPHETAMINE ("ICE") SMOKING PIPES

Methamphetamine Smoking Pipes

A commercial auto air freshener is emptied and the end of the tube is heated and blown into, creating a bulge at the end. A hole is poked through the bulging end with a hot needle.

METHAMPHETAMINE ("ICE") SMOKING PIPES

The end of a light bulb is cut off and the insides discarded. A hole is poked in the round end with a hot needle

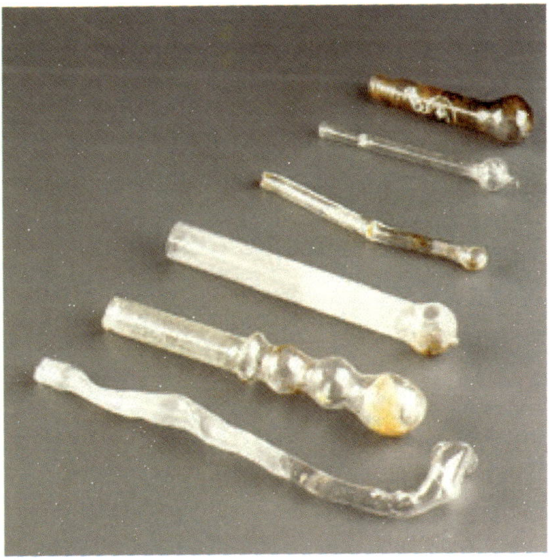

A small piece of the drug is placed inside the round portion of the pipe. The round portion is then heated from beneath, which causes creates vapors. There is a small hole at the top of the round portion of the pipe. The user places a finger over the hole, allowing the vapors to accumulate. The finger is then removed and the vapor is drawn into the lungs. Meth smokers often have a round burn mark on the finger used to block the bowl.

FOIL

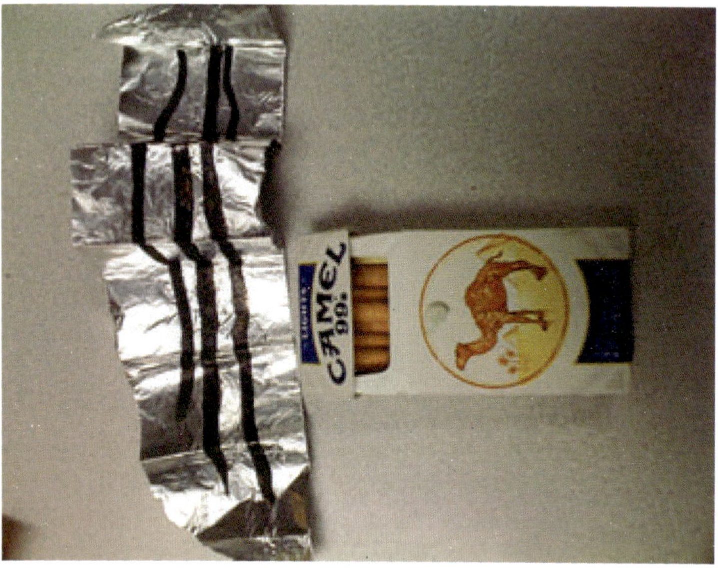

Foil used to smoke opiate-based pills. The black marks are from the burning pill streaking across the foil.

BINDLE

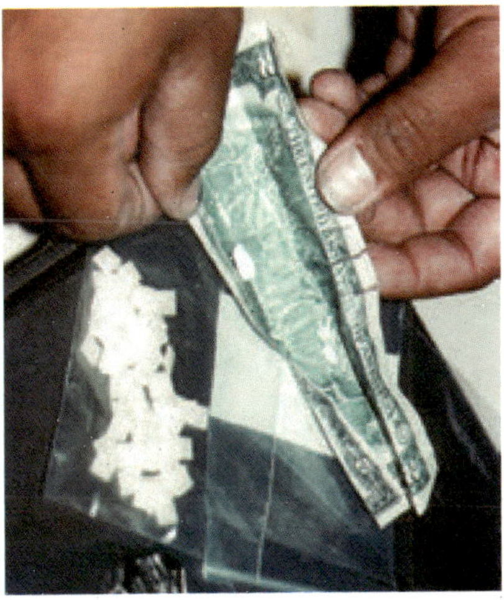

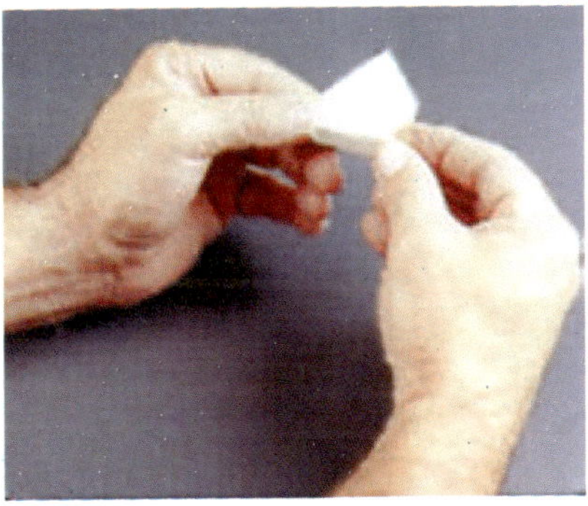

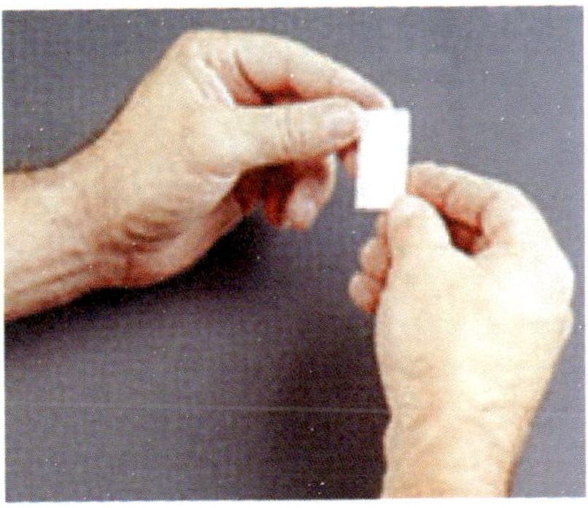

A bindle is a small piece of paper or currency, folded like an envelope to form a pocket, used to hold a personal amount of a drug.

COCAINE SIFTER

The drug is placed in the top compartment. The lid is screwed on and the handle is turned, forcing the powder through the screen. The result is a powder with a very fine texture for snorting.

SNORTING COCAINE

Powdered cocaine is placed on a mirror, piece of glass or other flat, non-porous surface. If not already in fine powder, it may be chopped with a razor blade or credit card. It is then combed into fine lines with the razor or credit card...

...the lines are then snorted through a tube such as a straw or rolled paper or dollar bill. It may also be snorted with a small spoon.

COPPER SCOURING PADS

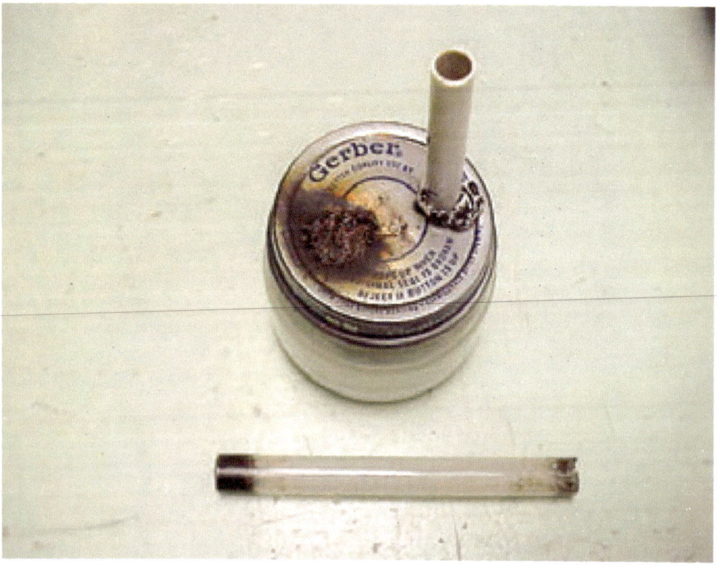

Small, round pieces of these pads are placed in bowls of Freebase Pipes. The "rock" is then placed on top of the pad and lit. The metal fibers of the pad hold the melting "rock" and keep it hot. The most popular brand of copper is "Chore Boy". Very fine steel wool or "Brillo pads" are also used.

DRUG LAB

Methamphetamine Lab

Typical Items Found at a Meth Lab

Methamphetamine can be made by a variety of recipes and methods. Simple methods render small quantities and more elaborate productions result in huge quantities. Bottom line, though, the main ingredients are common in households and stores, ephedrine or psuedoephedrine pills, Coleman cooking fuel, lithium batteries (the lithium is removed from the case and is highly flammable), etc.

HEROIN PARAPHERNALIA

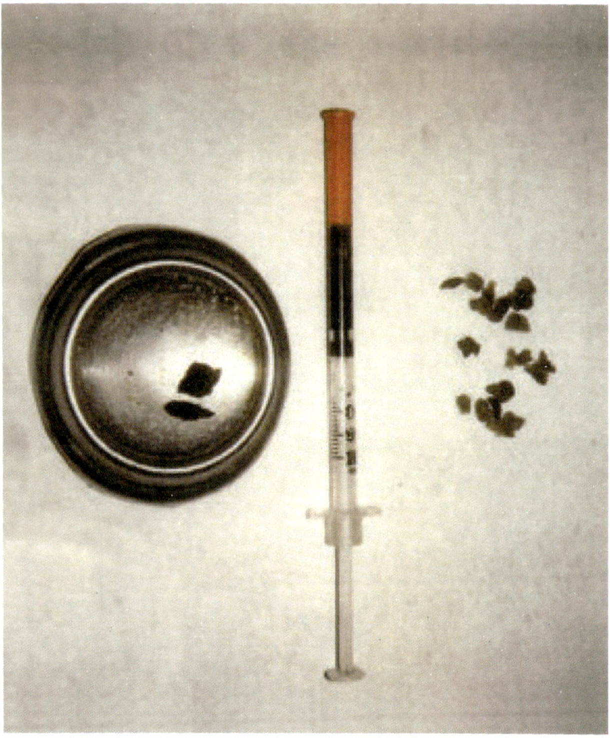

Powdered or Tar Heroin is placed in the "cooker", water is added, and solution is heated. A piece of cotton is added to act as a filter and the solution is drawn up into the needle. The arm is then "tied-off" with a belt, cord, or bandana to bulge the vein. The bulging of the vein is for easy injection and to cause the "rush" after the "tie-off" is released. The "cooker" is most often made from a spoon or bottom of an aluminum drink can.

This injection process is the same for Cocaine and/or Methamphetamine injections except the drugs are not heated because they are water soluble. They are placed in the cooker and warm water is added.

The "cottons" are kept. When the user does not have drugs, he will use the "cottons" to extract what ever small amount of Heroin is left in them. Cottons are considered drug residue and are not against the law to possess in some states.

NITROUS OXIDE PARAPHERNALIA

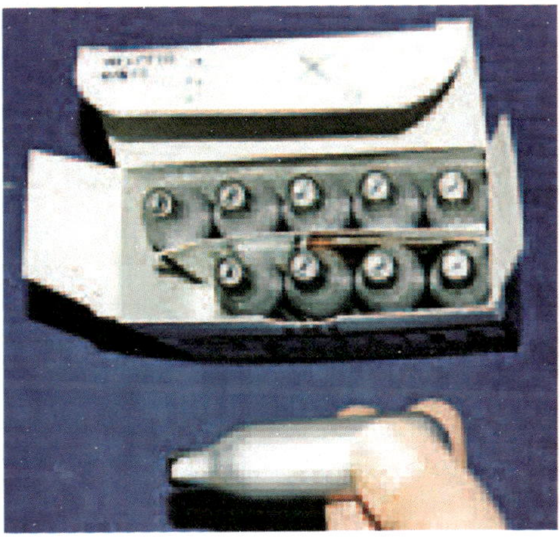

Nitrous Oxide Whippits

Nitrous oxide canisters (smaller than CO2 cylinders) are common in gourmet coffee shops because they propel the whipped cream from homemade whipped cream containers. Nitrous can be abused from the store's whipped cream makers just as it can from commercial cans of whipped cream (holding the can down releases whipped cream, holding it up releases the propellant, nitrous oxide). Employees have been known to slip a canister or two in the bottom of a large cup and then double cup the drink to send nitrous out with a friend.

Continued on the next page.

NITROUS OXIDE PARAPHERNALIA

Balloon & Cracker with Nitrous Oxide Cartridge

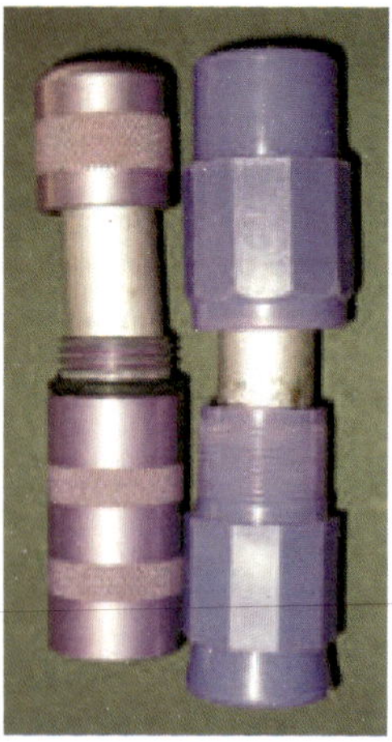

"Crackers" are devices used to puncture the whippets and fill balloons with nitrous oxide to then inhale. Most are aluminum or brass and the manufacturing quality resembles flashlights used by police. But they also come in plastic and can be made from standard PVC fittings (described on the Internet). The balloons are heavy duty, not typical party balloon quality. With the larger tanks of nitrous oxide (from dental offices, dental supply houses or the medium size from high performance vehicle shops), abusers may use the top half of a 2-liter soda bottle as an inhalation mask, attaching it to the tank with a piece of tubing. Inhaling directly from the tanks is dangerous as nitrous oxide gets very cold and can cause damage to lungs, etc. from the intense cold.

ECSTASY PARAPHERNALIA

MDMA (Ecstasy) enhances all of the senses, making everything pleasurable, including loud noises (users will cling to the speakers for the sound and vibration), touch (may fondle ordinary surfaces and find them fascinating), smell (love the smell of methanol chest rubs to enhance the act of breathing), sights (fascinated by flashing lights, for example), etc.

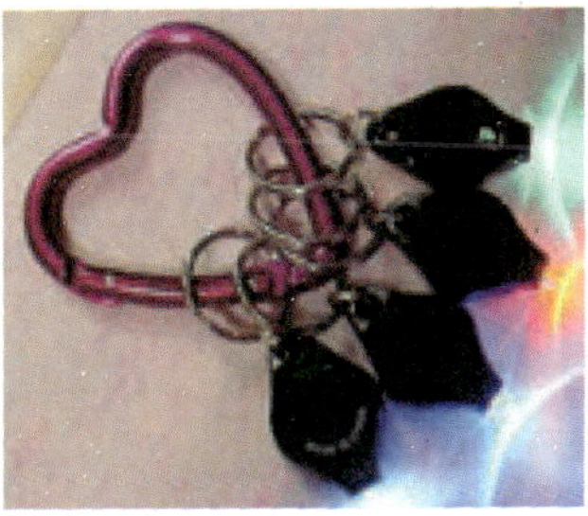

Ravers give each other "light shows" with various spinning or flashing lights. Using the photon lights, visible up to one mile, in their eyes at close proximity may cause damage.

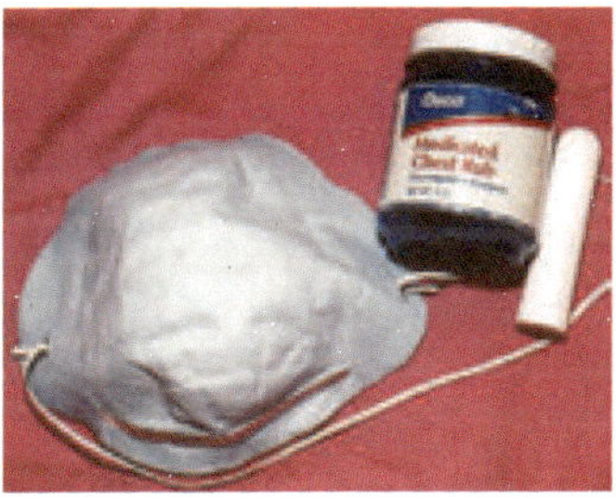

Vibrators, massages, the odor of vapor rub enhances their pleasure.

Continued on the next page.

ECSTASY PARAPHERNALIA

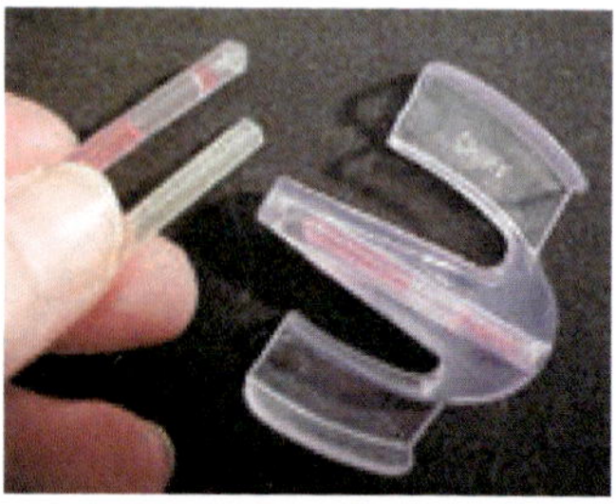

MDMA causes bruxism, teeth grinding; users suck on lollipops, pacifiers, glow sticks, etc., to try to reduce the teeth grinding and jaw locking.

Rave flyers are coded with images or phrases familiar to them and often overlooked by police, teachers and parents. The flyer doesn't say ONE, it says, "On Ecstasy;" Note the lower case "o" and "n" but the capital "E." C and E Flip refers to the flip (practice of mixing MDMA with another drug) of using both LSD and MDMA. "E" or "X" will be highlighted, underlined, capitalized, etc., to accentuate it.

Regular containers may be used to hide their drugs. PEZ containers may harbor MDMA pills or may contain actual PEZ candy laced with liquid LSD. MDMA pills may be found pressed into Tootsie Roll candies to get them past the eyes of teachers, cops and parents. These have also been used to smuggle black tar heroin into jail facilities. MDMA pills have been found intermingled with the candies on candy necklaces.

SCALES

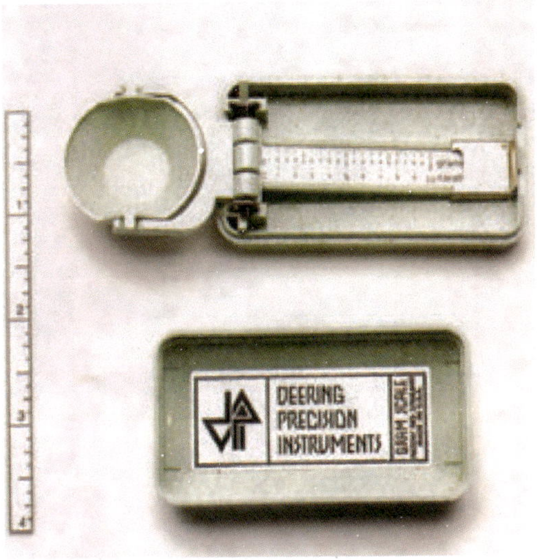

Pocket Scale Used for Weighing Drugs

Digital Scale used for Weighing Cocaine

These scales are often used by dealers who sell in small quantities (such as a gram). The dealers are often called "**Pocket Dealers**". The scale is assembled and the amount desired is set on the slide arm. The drug is then added to the bowl until the arm is level.

SNORTING SPOON

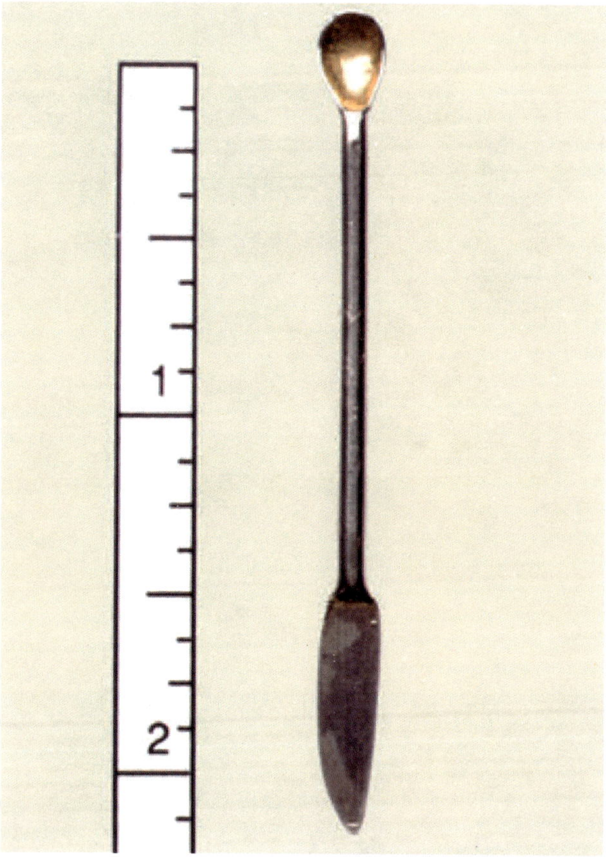

The desired amount of the drug is placed in the bowl of spoon (top in this photo). One nostril is closed while the other nostril is used to snort the drug from the spoon.

SNORTING TUBE

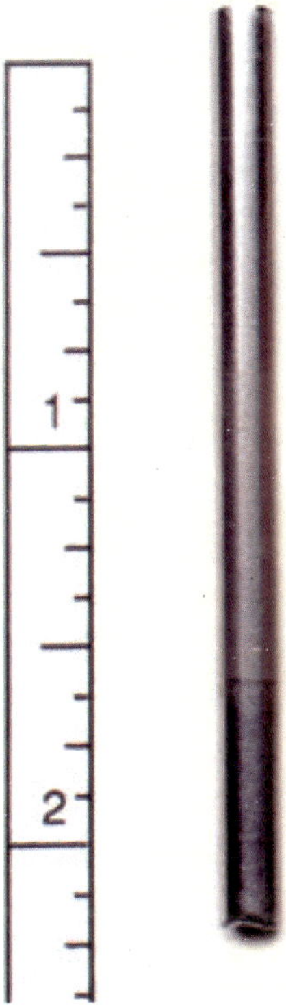

The desired amount of the drug is placed on a smooth surface, such as a piece of glass or a mirror. A razor blade or straight edge, such as a credit card, is used to chop the drug into fine particles. A "line" is then made with the substance. The tube is placed into one nostril while the other nostril is closed. The drug is then snorted through the tube into the nose. Snorting tubes may be made from glass or metal tubing. Often they are made from a tightly rolled twenty dollar bill, which results in the presence of drug residue on the bill.

SNORTING VIALS

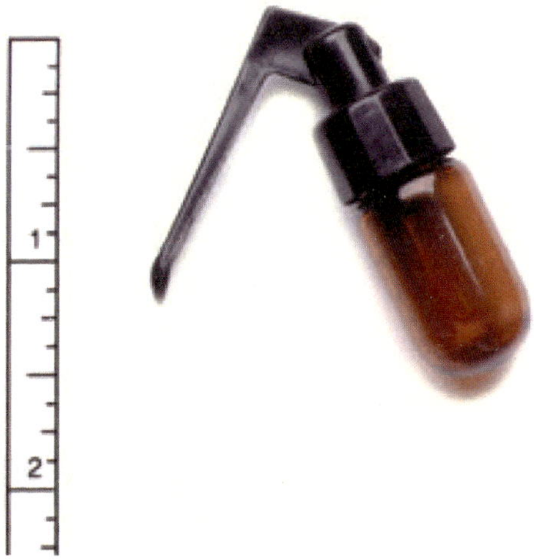

Continued on the next page.

SNORTING VIALS

The snorting vial consists of a small vial with a spoon-like device attached to the top. The drug is carried in the vial and a small amount is placed in the "spoon". One nostril is closed and the drug is snorted into the other nostril. In the device above, a small bowl is drilled into the top and the drug is snorted from that bowl.

STASH CANS

Continued on the next page.

STASH CANS

These cans are used to hold small quantities of drugs. Name brand product cans are modified to allow removal of the top or bottom end of the can. Threads may be "reversed" which makes the can appear normal when an attempt to unscrew the end by twisting in a counter-clockwise rotation. Stash cans may include beer or soft drink cans, aerosol containers, shaving cream cans or any number of other common household products.

WASH-BACK METHODS

As cocaine vapors travel the length of the pipe, some of the vapors dry and adhere to the sides of the pipe. The following processes are popular street methods for retrieving usable cocaine that is trapped inside the pipe.

WET WASH METHOD

A small amount of "151" rum is put into the mouthpiece of the pipe and the inside is washed out. The rum is then poured on a mirror or a piece of glass and ignited, burning off some of the rum. A piece of copper pad, Brillo pad or steel wool is rubbed on the glass to soak up what is left after burning. The pad is then placed in the pipe, lit, and the vapors drawn into the lungs.

DRY WASH METHOD

A small amount of "151" rum is put into the mouthpiece of the pipe and the inside is washed out. The rum is then poured on a mirror or a piece of glass and ignited. The rum is burned until it is completely dry. What is left on the glass or mirror is usable cocaine. This residue is scraped off the glass, placed in the pipe and smoked. The Dry Wash method is the most popular. These Wash-Back methods are primarily used with a freebase cocaine pipe, but may also be used with an "ice" or methamphetamine pipe.

CLOTHING INDICATES DRUG PREFERENCE

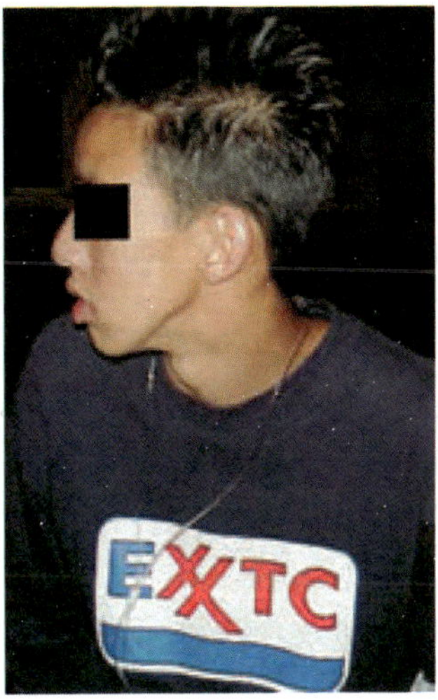

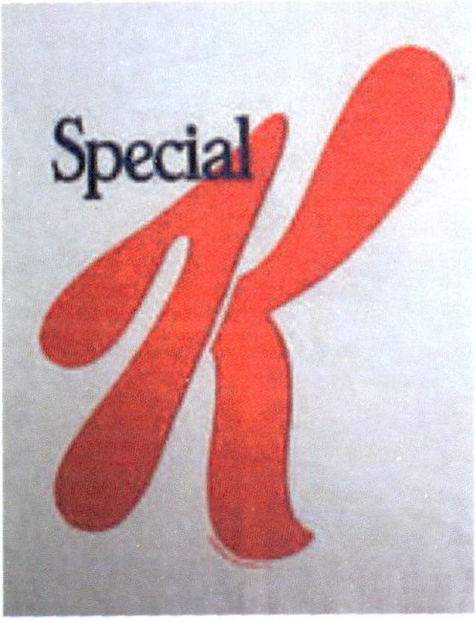

There is an endless stream of clothing and logos indicating drug preference and covers all drugs. Note the Ecstasy, Rated X and EXXTC, all indicating love for the drug MDMA. Special K refers to the animal tranquilizer ketamine. “420” stands for marijuana, April 20 being the universal beginning of the marijuana growing season.

CLOTHES THAT HIDE DRUGS

It isn't just in the hat band any more. Hats are made with hidden compartments in the area behind the logo, opening from inside the band with Velcro. Others have entire top sections with Velcro entry on the inside.

Continued on the next page.

CLOTHES THAT HIDE DRUGS

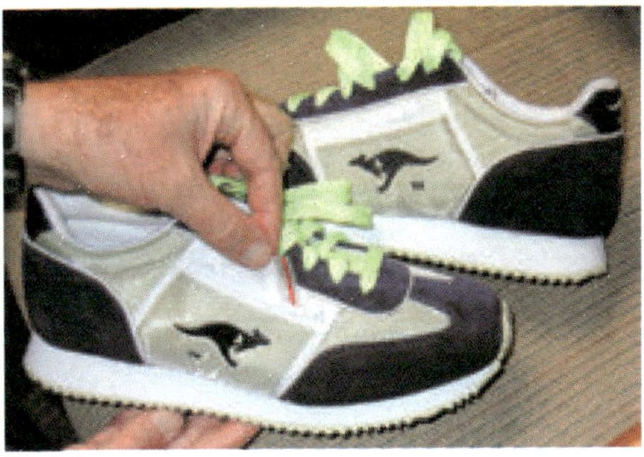

These items are innocent in themselves but it is important to do a thorough search and anticipate unusual hiding spots. Shoes have been found with carved-out areas in the sole, under the insert (commercially made as well as homemade) and in the side zip pockets (styles/brands common for kids and large enough for little more than a key or small quantities of dope. One pair was found at a rave with a zipper completely around the tongue, opening to a large compartment.

CLOTHES THAT HIDE DRUGS

Shirts and pants also come with numerous hidden features. Caffeine brand clothing features the "e" at the end backwards in their logo, similar to the concept of "flipping E," meaning doing the drug Ecstasy with other drugs—poly drug use. Caffeine and Kikwear clothing brands cater to the rave crowd. Velcro pockets may be found in the side seams or hem of shirts and pants. Some pants feature a hidden Velcro compartment on the inner leg seam, for example.

NEEDLE INJECTIONS AND PUNCTURE WOUNDS

STERILE INJECTIONS

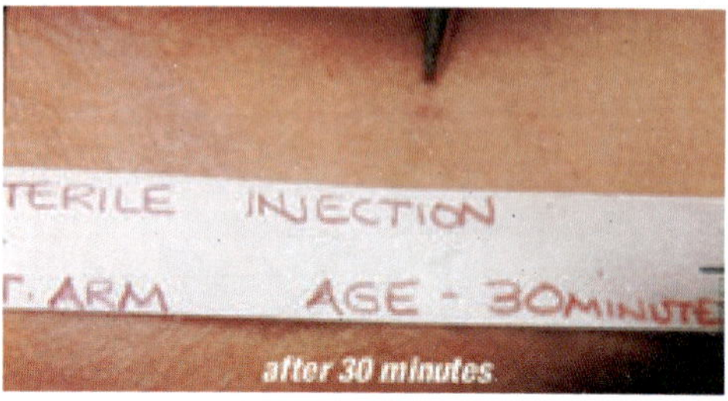

after 30 minutes

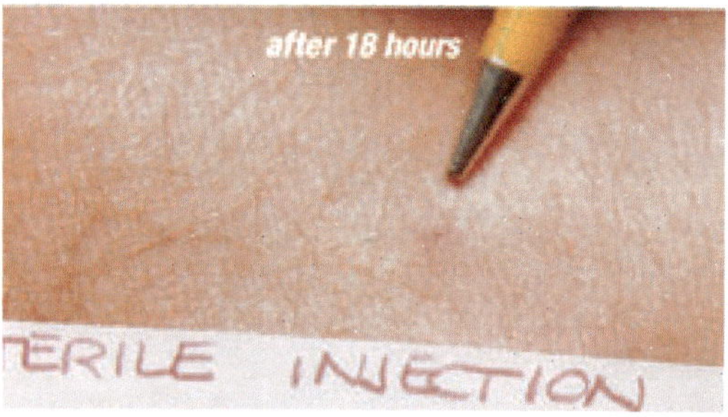

after 18 hours

NON-STERILE INJECTIONS

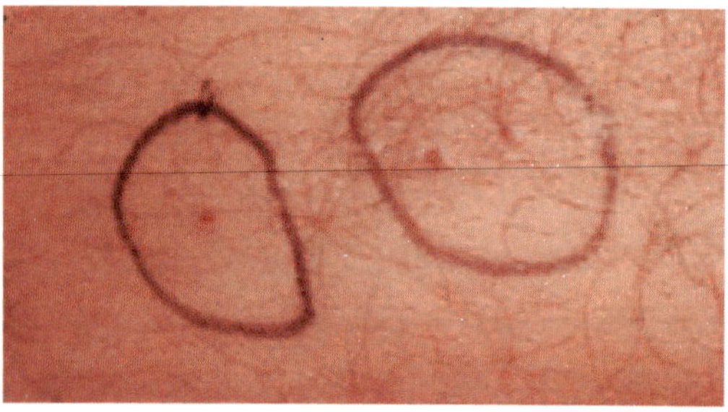

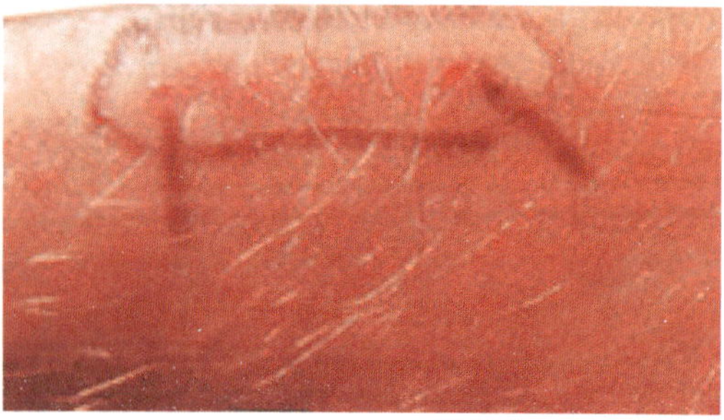

NEEDLE INJECTIONS

Heroin addicts prefer injecting directly into the vein for the most rapid, intense high. Physicians, on the other hand, most commonly inject narcotics under the skin or in muscle. The addict will inject virtually anywhere, either to attempt to hide the marks from view or because the scarring that builds up from chronic use necessitates venturing far and wide to find injection sites. They typically start with the arm and back of the hand but eventually may use ankles, calves, thighs, the groin area, lower portion of the lip, etc. Done properly and with sterile equipment, the injection site will be minor and heal quickly. But most heroin addicts have marks, scabs, abscesses and scar tissue over their veins from repeated injections under non-sterile, non-hygienic circumstances.

After the "fix" a small pinkish swelling will occur at the injection point. The swelling may appear as a tiny hole and may have fresh blood around it. Within 24 hours an infection may set in from non-sterile conditions. After a day so, the clotting blood and body serums form an orange-pink scab. The first scab would be slightly smaller than the head of a pin, round in shape with raised pink tissue in the center. There may be a bruised area around it if the user is inexperienced or careless. There may be an elongated area if a dull or bent needle was used. If the needle was dirty, there may be a black or blue tinge from the dirt or soot from the needle having been heated with a match. The surrounding tissue may be reddened and could have significant swelling. Two or three days later, the scab will become more orange and swelling reduced. The scab darkens as it ages. After about ten days the scab may flake off. There may be multiple marks of about the same age if the user injects repeatedly throughout the day or misses and has to try again. If the same site is used repeatedly, the scab will be larger and the area more traumatized. Scarring can become significant, forming visible "tracks" of the users historical injection sites. Abscesses may form from the unsanitary conditions and veins can collapse from the ongoing abuse.

Over the years, fear of needles and the growing risk of contracting HIV and other diseases made heroin abuse less attractive to the younger and richer set. But the availability of smokable, black tar heroin caused an increase in heroin abuse in wider circles.

This page intentionally left blank.

APPENDIX

AUTOEROTIC ASPHYXIATION, THE CHOKING GAME & CUTTING

Description:

These are practices gaining attention and perhaps increasing in the United States. The desired result is similar to the practice of inhaling—cutting off oxygen to the brain, for as little as sixty seconds, to produce a brief, euphoric altered state of consciousness that some people find pleasurable.

Autoerotic Asphyxiation is the act of masturbating and simultaneously choking oneself or being choked into a state of unconsciousness, enhancing sensation. "Erotic Asphyxiation" refers to couples choking each other during sexual acts for enhancement. This is a dangerous practice as the asphyxiation may go too far, resulting in injury or death.

The Choking Game has become increasingly popular among youth and is somewhat similar to inhalant abuse as it provides a brief euphoric experience. It's the younger version of sexual practice noted above. They call it things like, "fainting each other" or "dreaming." It produces a brief high and can cause brain damage or death. Indicators are unusual marks around the neck; ties, ropes or belts in unusual configurations; complaints of headaches; blood shot eyes.

Cutting or self-mutilation or other forms of self-harm is the act of seeking an altered mood state by inflicting harm serious enough to cause tissue damage to one's own body. It is a non-verbal means of dealing with overwhelming feelings or situations.

DRUG-FACILITATED SEXUAL ASSAULTS

Drug-Facilitated Sexual Assault (DFSA) is an offender's use of "anesthesia- type" drugs or hallucinogens, whether given stealthily or not, to render a subject physically helpless or otherwise incapacitated and thus incapable of giving or withholding consent. Voluntary intoxication does NOT equal consent to have sex, though it does represent risky behavior and leave the person more vulnerable to assault. The various drugs used in DFSA have a variety of effects with the most-prevalent being intoxication, amnesia, sleepiness or unconsciousness, and general inability to control their environment. The victim may be unconscious during all or part of act, and may have amnesia even when conscious and appearing to function and "participate" at some stages.

More than 50 different drugs have been used to facilitate sexual assault (and may also be used in robbery). Predatory drugs include these types of drugs:

- Alcohol
- GHB or its "analogs" GBL, BD and others
- Benzodiazepines, such as flunitrazepam (roofies, Rohypnol), Ativan, Xanax, etc.
- Other sedative-hypnotics, such as ketamine, PCP
- Sleeping pills, such as Ambien
- Muscle relaxants, such as Soma, Flexeril
- Antihistamines, such as diphenhydramine (as in Benadryl)
- Animal tranquilizers, such telazol
- Motion sickness/nausea prevention pills, such as scopalomine
- Narcotic analgesics
- MDMA & other hallucinogens

Urine is the sample of choice in DFSA cases and should be obtained as soon as possible, as some of these drugs dissipate from the body rapidly. GHB, for example, is in the blood for only four hours and in the urine for only 12.

Absence of a drug in toxicology results alone does not mean that a drug rape has not occurred. Consider the timing of the event—the time from the suspected drink or food and the time when the sample was finally obtained. A negative toxicology result may merely reflect that the sample was taken after the drug dissipated. The victim's statements, observations by witnesses, etc., may help to establish that a drug, and which drug type, was likely used. Some state laws do not require a positive test result proving a specific drug but may be prosecuted based on effects, observed symptoms, etc. Screening tests may NOT detect all drugs. Confirmation testing should be done when circumstances indicate a possible DFSA and the drug screen is negative.

DRUG STATISTICS

Total of All Meth Clandestine Laboratory Incidents Including Labs, Dumpsites, Chem/Glass/Equipment Calendar Year 2012

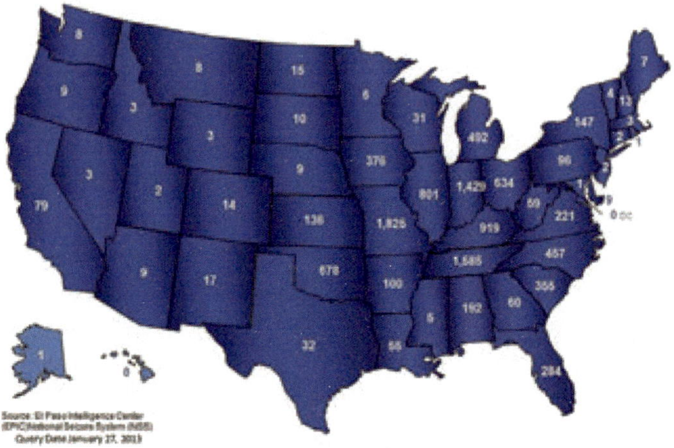

Source: El Paso Intelligence Center (EPIC) National Seizure System (NSS)

Total: 11,210

Dates: 01/01/2012 - 12/31/2012

Drug Enforcement Administration Heroin Signature Program

The DEA operates the Heroin Signature Program (HSP), using scientific profiling to identify the origin of heroin seized and purchased in the United States. DEA chemists can determine which of the world's four major heroin producing regions was the source of the drug. These regions are: South America, Mexico, Southeast Asia and Southwest Asia. HSP data is used in conjunction with investigative intelligence and with production and seizure data to develop an overall assessment of heroin trafficking to and within the United States. More information is available at the DEA website: **www.dea.gov**.

EARLY WARNING SIGNS

Early Warning Signs of Adolescent Drug Abuse

There are numerous early warning signs of adolescent drug abuse. In order to detect the early warning signs, keep an open line of communication and be aware, observant, and open-minded. Drug abuse infiltrates all social, economic, and cultural structures. The current national average of the onset of drug and alcohol use is under 13 years of age.

Early Warning Signs:

- A distinctive change in attitude, usually a negative change.
- Decline in school work and grades.
- Poor school attendance, frequent Monday and Friday absences.
- Distinctive change in friends.
- Distinctive change in clothing.
- Distinctive change in taste of music and movies.
- Disciplinary problems a home and school.
- Isolation from friends.
- Mood swings.
- Outbursts of violence (physical and/or verbal).
- Discovery of drugs, drug paraphernalia, or drug publications.
- Distinctive change in appearance. (Examples: tattoos, ear rings, nose rings, etc.)
- Noticeable decrease in motivation and enthusiasm.
- Abandonment of areas of interest or hobbies.
- Stealing (inside and outside the home).
- Marked increase of physical illness.

GATEWAY DRUGS

Gateway drugs are most commonly used by adolescents. These drugs are:

- Alcohol
- Inhalants
- Marijuana
- Prescription medication
- Tobacco (including smokeless)

Adolescence is the life stage between childhood and adulthood. The onset of gateway drug use was considered to be around age 12 yrs., but is often younger. Adolescents use the so-called gateway drugs due to the fact they are readily available and inexpensive. These chemicals can cause inhibition of growth and abnormal emotional development. They reason they are called gateway drugs is that they can lead the adolescent down the path toward other illicit drug abuse.

More recently MDMA (Ecstasy) has become a major gateway drug and rave parties are often a "gateway event" for the young. The first drug they are exposed to—whatever drug that is—may be the gateway, opening the door to other drug exposure and usage. Parents may serve as the gateway, especially with alcohol, tobacco and today with methamphetamine.

DRUG FIELD EVALUATION

HORIZONTAL GAZE NYSTAGMUS TEST

Smooth Pursuit

While the subject is looking straight ahead, place a stimulus (index finger) 15 inches in front of the tip of the nose and even with the eyebrows. Move the stimulus (index finger) to the subject's left about 45 degrees watching for an involuntary jerking of the eyes. Proceed to move the stimulus (index finger) to the right eye and repeat procedure. Do this twice with each eye. When moving the stimulus (index finger) to the left, check the left eye.

When moving the stimulus (index finger) to the right, check the right eye. Move the stimulus (index finger) straight across in front of the subject's face.

Maximum Deviation

Administer this test in the exact same manner as the Smooth Pursuit Test except at the 45 degrees, hold the stimulus (index finger) still for 5 seconds. Look for involuntary jerking of the eye.

Additional Comments:

Some people have nystagmus naturally.

VERTICAL GAZE NYSTAGMUS TEST

With the subject looking straight ahead, place the stimulus (index finger) 15 inches out from the tip of the nose. Move stimulus (index finger) upward level with the top of the head and down to the tip of the nose. Do this test at least twice looking at each eye once. Record your results.

Note: Vertical Nystagmus is when the eyeballs jerk vertically (up and down).

LACK OF CONVERGENCE TEST

When the subject is looking straight ahead, place the stimulus (index finger) 15 inches in front of the tip of the nose. First move the stimulus in front of the face counter clockwise. The circles should not be larger than the subject's face.

When you are sure the subject is following the stimulus with his eyes, bring the stimulus (index finger) to the nose and touch the bridge of the nose. Tell the subject to watch the stimulus (index finger) on the bridge of the nose for at least 5 seconds. Look for either or both eyes drifting outward, not being able to focus inward on the nose.

Additional Comments:

Non-convergence can be natural in some individuals.

ROMBERG 30 SECOND ESTIMATION OF TIME

During the explanation and demonstration of this test, have the subject stand upright with heels and toes together and their hands at their sides. This is the "Romberg Position."

Test: In the "Romberg Position," have the subject tilt his head back and close his eyes. When you say begin, have the subject estimate 30 seconds. (This should be done silently.) When the subject believes the 30 seconds are finished, he should open his eyes and bring his head forward. This indicates the end of the test. If the subject has not completed the test in 90 seconds, discontinue the test.

Additional Comments:

- Drugs that speed up the body will cause a short estimation of time (cocaine, amphetamines, etc.), and the drugs that slow the system down will cause a long estimation of time (depressants, narcotics, alcohol, etc.).
- Be aware of the actual time during the test. Note body movements such as swaying, body tremors, muscle rigidity, etc.
- Make sure the subject performs the test as instructed.

PUPIL/LIGHT ACCOMMODATION TEST

The purpose of this series of tests is to examine the reaction, or lack of reaction, to the presence and absence of light. Use a pen light and a Pupilometer. (Average pupil size is 3.0 to 6.5 millimeters.)

Available Light

Using whatever light is available at the time of the test, use a Pupilometer to check the size of both pupils. Always check the left pupil first (to keep the test standardized and systematic) and note the size of each pupil separately. To do this, place the Pupilometer along the temple side of the eye. Locate the circle that best matches the size of the pupil and note that size. (Do not cover any portion of the eye with the Pupilometer during this test.)

Close to Total Darkness

Expose the subject's eyes to a minimum of 90 seconds of uninterrupted, total darkness. Next, place the pad of the index finger over the lens of the pen light. (This will result in a red light.) Place the Pupilometer on the temple side of the eye and shine the red light into the eye. Measure the size of the pupil, doing the left eye first (to keep the test standardized and systematic), then note the size of each pupil separately.

Direct Light

Shine the inner beam of the pen light directly into the eye. Position the beam of light between the eyebrows and the top of the cheekbone. Hold the light in this position for one minute. Measure the size of the pupil of the left eye first (to standardize test) with the Pupilometer. Note the measurement of each pupil separately.

STANDARD FIELD SOBRIETY TESTS

The following is an explanation of the four standardized field sobriety tests. Please keep in mind:

- These tests should be used for ALL driving-under-the-influence situations, not just for alcohol intoxication.
- Give clear instructions to the subject and be sure they understand what is required of them before they begin each test.
- Conduct each test on a flat surface that is well-lighted and void of any obstructions.
- Discontinue any test if the subject is in any danger of injury.
- Take complete notes as you administer each test.
- These tests should be given in the same order and instructed in the same way each time to standardize the tests.

WALK-AND-TURN

During the explanation and demonstration, have the subject place his right foot on the line he will be walking on. Then have him place the toes of his left foot against the heel of his right foot. Standing flat on the ground with both feet pointing in the same direction, stand up straight with both arms at his side.

Test: After assuming the above position, instruct the subject to walk nine steps up the line, turn around and walk nine steps back. (Each step should be heel to toe.) The subject will look down at his feet and count each step out loud. At the end of the first nine steps, the subject will turn. (The turn will be a three-point pivot), keeping the front foot in its place and using the balls of this foot to pivot.) With the back foot, push three times around to face the opposite direction. Walk back nine steps in the same manner. If at any time the subject falls off the line, he is to regain his balance and continue to walk and count off his steps where he left off. Discontinue test if subject is in danger of injury.

Additional Comments:

- Note any difficulties balancing.
- Note if the subject uses his arms or any other object for balance.
- Be sure he touches heel to toe as instructed.
- Make sure the turn is done as instructed.
- The counting of steps should be loud enough to be heard.
- Make sure the subject performs the test as instructed.

ONE-LEG-STAND

During the explanation and demonstration, have the subject stand in the "Romberg Position." (Stand upright with heels and toes together, and hands at the side.)

Test: From the "Romberg Position," instruct the subject to first balance on his left leg by raising his right leg until his right foot is six inches off the ground. Have the subject point his toes down on the right foot, and while looking at his right foot, count to 30 out loud. (Have the subject count one thousand one, one thousand two, one thousand three, etc.) If at any time the subject loses his balance, he is to regain balance and continue counting where he left off. Discontinue test if subject is in danger of injury.

Additional Comments:

- Note if subject uses arms or any other object for balance.
- Note any difficulties in balancing.
- The subject must count correctly.
- Make sure the subject performs the test as instructed.

FINGER-TO-NOSE

During the explanation and demonstration, the subject should stand in the "Romberg Position." (Stand upright with heels and toes together, and hands at the side.) Have the subject make a fist with both hands and extend his index finger on each hand, then place his arms at his sides.

Test: From the above position, instruct the subject to tilt his head back and close his eyes. When instructed, the subject is to touch the tip of his index finger to the tip of his nose. After touching his nose, the subject will bring his hand down to the starting position without being told. The sequence of instruction is left, right, left, right, right, left.

Additional Comments:

- Note any body movements, such as swaying, body tremors, muscle rigidity, etc.
- Observe where the index finger touches the face.
- Make sure the subject performs the test as instructed.

DRUG TESTING

TYPES OF DRUG TESTING

Drug Screening

Drug screening is a simple, rapid, and easy test that can be used by a layperson. Drug screening tests give qualitative results (positive or negative) meaning that if positive, the drug is present above a certain level. They do not usually give quantitative results. Drug screenings tests can be done on urine and saliva. An example of a drug screening test being used by law enforcement would be an officer who makes a car stop and discovers that the driver could possibly be under the influence of a drug. After administering a DAR or DRE examination and determining if the driver is under the influence of a drug, the officer could use an oral fluid or urine drug screening test to confirm his determination immediately. Drug screening tests use specially designed drug strips to detect a drug and its metabolites in oral fluid or urine. The oral fluid or urine, once collected, can be sent to a confirmation lab to confirm the presences of the drug or its metabolites. Drug screening tests are sometimes referred to as Point of Care tests (POC).

Quantitative Analysis

To determine if a person is under the influence of drugs, a sample must be obtained from the suspect. The two most common ways to obtain evidence of drug use is by collecting a sample of blood or a sample of urine. A third method that is emerging is oral fluid (saliva). Each has its benefits.

Urine: Drugs will remain in the urine for much longer period of time (2 to 5 days) than in the blood or saliva. Most drugs take at least two hours to metabolize before they appear in the urine. For example, if you witness a woman smoking crack, you would have to wait a minimum of two hours before the cocaine will appear in a urine test. The same person, may be positive for cocaine for two or three days.

Blood: Blood tests are very accurate and indicate the level of drug in the body at that time. Drugs appear within a half hour after use, but have a shorter life span in the blood. Typically, most drug and metabolites will only stay for 8 hours in the blood. Blood test requires the specimen to be sent to a lab.

Saliva: Saliva is comparable to blood in many respects. The benefit of saliva as a drug testing option is the elimination of gender collection issues that exist with urine collection samples. It is much harder to taint a saliva sample (adulterate the sample), and officers can do it road side. Positive saliva tests indicate recent drug use.

UNDERSTANDING TOXICOLOGY RESULTS

Toxicology results can be confusing as they may be reported in a variety of concentration units. They may be reported as nanograms per milliliter (ng/mL). Other labs use micrograms per milliliter (µg/mL). There is a 1,000-time difference between nanograms and micrograms, making comparison and understand very confusing.

Units of Concentration Conversion

1 mg/L = 1 μg/mL

1 mg/mL = 1000 μg/mL

1 μg/mL = 1000 ng/mL

1 mg/dL = 10 μg/mL

100 μg/dL = 1 μg/mL

Detection Limits

Note: Times relate to length of time drugs can be detected in urine, except where blood limitations are specifically noted. Times are estimates and specific drugs within categories may vary.

Cocaine 2-3 days
Metabolite[1]

Cannabis
Single use 3 days
Moderate use (4 times/week) 5 days
Heavy use (daily) 10 days
Chronic heavy use21-27 days

Gamma Hydroxybutyrate (GHB & Analogs GBL & BD)
Urine 12 hours
Blood3-5 hours

Opiates. 48 hours
(including heroin, morphine, codeine)

PCP (Phencyclidine) 48 hours to 8 days

Amphetamines 48 hours
(including methamphetamines)

Benzodiazepines[2] 3 days, approx
(including diazepam/Valium, clonazepam/Klonopins, therapeutic dose)

---

1 A **metabolite** is the substance(s) produced by the body metabolizing (breaking down) a drug. Metabolites may by psychoactive or inactive, but are detectable in blood and urine and are often the basis for drug tests. For example, cocaine produces the metabolite benzoylecogonine; when cocaethylene (AKA: ethylcocaine) is detected, that indicates combined use of alcohol and cocaine. Presence of the parent drug, cocaine, indicates recent use. Some drugs, such as PCP,A are detected only as the drug itself, with no metabolites.

2 There is a wide range of benzodiazepine drugs available and some may not be readily detectable in a "drug screen" (i.e. immunoassay) in either blood or urine, such as lorazepam (Ativan), alprazolam (Xanax) and triazolam (Halcion). Other testing procedures should be used before ruling out the presence of benzos.

Barbiturates

Short acting (secobarbital)	24 hours
Intermediate acting	48-72 hours
Long acting (phenobarbital)	7 days or more
Phenobarbital	24 hours (blood)

Propoxyphene (Darvon)

Unchanged	6 hours
Metabolite	6-48 hours

WEIGHTS & MEASURES

Dry Measures

1 Microgram (mcg) = 1/1000 of a Milligram (mg)

1000 Micrograms (mcg) = 1 Milligram (mg)

1000 Grams = 1 Kilogram (kilo.)

1 Kilogram (kilo.) = 2.2 Pounds (lbs)

1 Gram (g) = 15.43 Grains (gr.)

28.35 Grams (g) = 1 Ounce (oz)

453.6 Grams (g) = 1 Pound (lb)

1 Grain (gr) = 65 Milligrams (mg)

1 Grain (gr) = 0.065 Grams (g)

1 Ounce (oz) = 437.5 Grains (gr)

1 Ounce (oz) = 28.3 Grams (g)

1 Ounce (oz) = 28,350 Milligrams (mg)

1 Ounce (oz) = Approximately 6 Tablespoons (tbls)

1 Pound (lbs) = 7,000 Grains

1 Pound (lbs) = 16 Ounces

1 Pound (lbs) = 453 Grams (g)

1 Ton = 2,000 Pounds (lbs)

Liquid Measures

1 L (Liter) = approximately one quart

1000ml (milliliters) = 1 Liter

Additional Comments:

For comparison purposes and for training, one gram equals one packet of sugar substitute, such as Sweet N Low®.

DRUG ABUSE IN THE WORKPLACE

Statistics:

- An estimated 70% of all individuals abusing drugs are employed.
- The abuse of alcohol and other drugs is costing American business owners over one hundred billion dollars ($100,000,000,000) annually due to insurance rate increases, workman's compensation, etc.
- Drug use shows up at all levels in the workplace, from professionals to unskilled workers.
- An estimated 20% of the workplace population is using alcohol or other drugs at the work-site.
- Almost 60% of the world's production of illegal drugs are consumed in the United States while only 5% of the world's population is located in the United States.

Abusers In The Workplace:

- Are less productive.
- Miss several days of work.
- Are more likely to injure themselves or someone else.
- File more worker's compensation claims.
- Are more likely to steal from employer and/or co-workers.
- A cause of low morale among co-workers.
- Cause an increase in co-worker's work load.
- Cause insurance rates to increase.

Recognizing Abusers In The Workplace:

- Accidents on the job.
- Frequent absences and/or late to work.
- Frequent mistakes that require additional work to correct.
- Uncharacteristic behavior (moodiness, giddiness, violent threats, etc.).
- Obsessed with drugs and alcohol and trying to get others to participate.

Fighting Drug Abuse In The Workplace

- The best way to fight drug abuse in the workplace is through a five part program.
- A written substance abuse policy.
- An employee education & awareness program.
- Supervisor training program.
- An employee assistance program.
- Drug testing when appropriate.

WORKPLACE DRUG ABUSE RESOURCES

Workplace Drug Training
www.gravesassociates.com
1 (888) 536-3494

California Narcotic Officers' Association
1 (877) 775-6272
www.cnoa.org

Drug-Free Workplace Helpline
1 (800) 967-5752
beta.samhsa.gov/workplace

National Clearinghouse for Alcohol & Drug Information
1 (800) 729-6686

Substance Abuse and Mental Health Services Administration (SAMHSA)
Treatment Helpline & Facilities Locator
1 (800) 662-4357
beta.samhsa.gov/find-help

RESOURCES FOR DRUG PREVENTION

www.projectghb.org

www.taylorhooton.org

www.couragetospeak.org

www.notMYkid.org

www.dammad.org

www.painfullyobvious.com

www.teens.drugabuse.gov

www.theantidrug.com

www.drugfree.org

www.justthinktwice.com

This page intentionally left blank.

DEFINITIONS

ANABOLIC STEROID Medically used to some extent but also personally abused to promote muscle growth and tissue development. Typically abused by athletes but increased use has been seen among teens to overcome harassment for being small, skinny and by young females to be more firm and lean. Users run the risk of increased cancer, acne and other negative side effects. Many counterfeit products are also being distributed.

ANALGESIC Drugs that relieve pain, such as codeine, zolpidem, oxycodone, etc.

ANALOG Chemical cousin of another drug, with similar properties and related chemical structure (definition for legal purposes varies from state to state). This is the basis for "designer drug" issues, where a chemist may alter the structure of an illegal substance, seeking a drug of similar properties for abuse purposes but not yet illegal. But, when and where analog laws apply (and depending on the precise wording), the new substance may be automatically covered and made illegal for human consumption.

ATAXIA Loss of muscle coordination.

CNS Central Nervous System.

HYPERTHERMIA Over-heating of the body due to certain drug effects or disease. Defined as body temperature over 104 degrees. Drugs associated with this include MDMA, LSD, amphetamines, cocaine, PCP, etc.

HYPOTHERMIA Decreased body temperature due to exposure to cold, certain drug effects. Defined as body temperature below 90 degrees. Drugs associated with this include barbiturates, ethanol, GHB, sedative-hypnotics, opiates, etc.

SINSEMILLA Seedless marijuana.

SYNESTHESIA The effect of drugs such as LSD in which the user's sensory system is crossed, resulting in the "seeing" sounds, "hearing" colors, etc.

TACHYCARDIA Excessive heart rate (pulse greater than 100).

STREET SLANG

Varies greatly from city to city, state to state, culture to culture, etc. We have attempted to gather the most commonly used language.

2-CI Emerging street drug 2,5-dimethoxy-4-iodophenethy-lamine (See TRYPTAMINE).

2-CB Street drug 4-bromo-2,5-dimethoxyphenethylamine (See NEXUS, BROMO).

2C-T-7 Street drug 2,5-dimethoxy-4-(n)-propylthiophenethyl- amine known as Tripstasy, Lucky 7, 7-Up (See LUCKY 7).

8-TRACK Street gang term meaning 2.5 grams of Cocaine.

ABE Five dollars worth of a drug.

ABSINTHE Typically green liquor of grain alcohol and wormwood (artemesia absinthium), with a high alcohol content plus the chemical thujone.

ACAPULCO GOLD A particularly potent form of Marijuana grown in the Acapulco area (See GOLD and GOLD LEAF).

ACCESSORIES Drug paraphernalia.

ACE

a. A Marijuana cigarette (See JOINT)
b. PCP

ACETONE A chemical that is mainstay of many illicit drug preparations, making it a regulated chemical; can also be abused as an inhalant.

ACID LSD (Lysergic Acid Diethylamide).

ACID CUBE A sugar cube containing LSD.

ACID FREAK A heavy regular user of LSD.

ACID HEAD LSD user.

ACK-ACK Method by which Heroin/Cocaine is smoked on the tip of a burning cigarette.

ACTION To use or sell drugs.

AD A drug addict.

ADAM Slang for the drug MDMA (3,4-Methylenedioxy-NMethylamphetamine).

ADAM & EVE IN THE GARDEN OF EDEN Polydrug abuse, called a flip, taking MDMA with the drugs MDEA and MBDB, all at the same time (See FLIP).

AFGHANI Drugs from Afghanistan. Usually Marijuana.

AMF Slang for the drug Alpha-Methylfentanyl.

AMPED High on amphetamines.

AMBIEN Sleeping pill containing Zolpidem that can be abused or used for drugging for rape or robbery.

AMT/A-MT Alpha-methyl-tryptamine is another drug being seen in pill or powder form, typically in same clientele as MDMA; also called Spirals, Amtrak or Amthrax (See TRYPTAMINE).

AMYL NITRATE A prescription drug for coronary artery disease that is also abused by inhaling the fumes, giving a brief but intense rush (See POPPERS, BUTYL NITRATE).

ANABOLIC STEROID Medically used to some extent but also personally abused to promote muscle growth and tissue development; typically abused by athletes but increased use has been seen among teens to overcome harassment for being small, skinny and by young females to be more firm and lean; users run the risk of increased cancer, acne and other negative side effects; many counterfeit products are also being distributed.

ANALGESIC Drugs that relieve pain, such as codeine, zolpidem, oxycodone, etc.

ANALOG Chemical cousin of another drug, with similar properties and related chemical structure (definition for legal purposes varies from state to state); this is the basis for "designer drug" issues, where a chemist may alter the structure of an illegal substance, seeking a drug of similar properties for abuse purposes but not yet illegal; when and where analog laws apply (and depending on the precise wording), the new substance may be automatically covered and made illegal for human consumption.

ANGEL DUST

a. Phencyclidine (PCP)
b. PCP sprinkled on Marijuana in powdered form and smoked

ANGEL'S TRUMPET The Datura plant, a hallucinogen, is also called Angel's Trumpet or Devil Weed or Jimson Weed (See DATURA).

ANIMAL TRANK PCP.

ARNOLD Street term for anabolic steroid.

ARTILLERY Drug paraphernalia for injecting.

ASTRO TURF Marijuana.

ATROPINE From datura and belladonna plants, atropine has legitimate medical uses but abuse can produce hallucinations, severe toxic effects and even death.

AUTHOR A doctor or anyone who writes illegal prescriptions.

BABYSITTER An individual knowledgeable about the effects of hallucinogens, particularly in the case of LSD. The babysitter provides reassurance and reality for the novice user (See CO-PILOT).

BACK-UP A procedure permitting blood back into the syringe to ensure that the needle is in a vein (a frequent precaution taken by veteran heroin addicts).

BAD TRIP An unpleasant, frightening or even terrifying experience occurring after the ingestion of a hallucinogenic drug or after ingestion of other drugs with hallucinogenic properties.

BAG A small container of a drug, usually just enough for personal use.

BALL Mexican Black Tar Heroin.

BALLOON A toy balloon used for packaging Mexican Powdered Heroin. The balloon is used to enable the possessor to swallow it if approached by the authorities. It is later retrieved after defecation.

BANG Injecting.

BARBS Barbiturates.

BARREL

a. A quantity of 100,000 pills
b. A particular shape of LSD tablet

BASA Spanish word for base.

BASE Freebased Cocaine.

BASEBALL Cocaine Freebase.

BASING The process of converting powdered Cocaine (Hydrochloride) into a purified solid for smoking.

BASUCO/BASA Raw Coca Paste directly from the Coca Plant. It is a dark paste that is smoked, usually by South American peasants.

BATU Hawaiian term for the large smokable crystals of Methamphetamine.

BAYONET Hypodermic syringe.

BC Bud Marijuana from British Columbia.

BEANS.

a. Dexedrine
b. More currently and commonly used to refer to MDMA pills, especially in Florida

BEAUTIFUL A drug of good quality, producing an exceptionally intense euphoria.

BEHIND STUFF Using heroin, as in "I'm behind stuff".

BELLY HABIT Addiction where withdrawals cause severe stomach cramps.

BELT

a. High or Euphoria produced by a drug high
b. To quickly consume alcohol
c. A large mouthful of alcohol.

BENNIES The prescription drug Benzedrine, however, it is no longer manufactured (See BENZ and DRIVERS).

BENT To be high on any drug.

BENZ The prescription drug Benzedrine, however, it is no longer manufactured (See BENNIES and DRIVERS).

BENZODIAZEPINES (AKA: BENZO) A group of depressant drugs typically for sleep or anxiety disorders, such as Valium, Xanax, Ativan (See DEPRESSANTS).

BERNICE Cocaine.

BETEL NUT From the areca palm tree, betel nut is commonly used in some Asian cultures and produces a mild stimulant effect.

BHANG Marijuana.

BIG CHIEF Peyote.

BIG C Cocaine.

BIG D LSD.

BIG H Heroin.

BIG MAN Upper level drug dealer.

BINDLE Paper used to hold a personal amount of a powdered drug. Folded like an envelope.

BINGE A sustained period of uninterrupted alcohol uses, sometimes refers to the same practice with other drugs.

BINKY or BINKIE Pacifiers used by abusers of the drug MDMA (Ecstasy) to reduce the bruxism (teeth grinding) that it often causes.

BLACK & WHITES Biphetamine that comes in a black & white capsule (See BLACK BEAUTIES).

BLACK BEAUTIES Biphetamine that comes in a black and white capsule (See BLACK & WHITES).

BLACK JACK Tincture of Opium cooked to a concentrated form and injected.

BLACK TAR HEROIN A form of Mexican Heroin.

BLANK An inert substance mixed with a drug to produce more of the substance for sales.

BLASTED An intense drug high.

BLAZING Smoking marijuana.

BLOND Gold or yellow colored solid Hashish from the Middle East (Lebanese Blond).

BLOTTER ACID Small squares of heavy stock paper, perforated for tearing, with a drop of LSD on each. Ingested orally. Sometimes there are pictures stamped on each one.

BLOW

a. Slang for Cocaine
b. Inhalation of smoke

BLOW A STICK (or JOINT) Smoking a marijuana joint.

BLOW THE VEIN Injecting a vein with too much of the substance usually causing the vein to collapse.

BLOW YOUR MIND To get high on a hallucinogenic.

BLOWING UP (or BLOWIN' UP) Getting high on MDMA (Ecstasy).

BLUE CHEER A combination of LSD, Methamphetamine, and Strychnine.

BLUE DEVILS Prescription drug Amytal Sodium in a blue capsule.

BLUE HEAVEN LSD.

BLUELIGHTER Refers to someone who participates in the on-line message board called bluelight, a common discussion ground for ravers and drug abusers (www.bluelight.nu).

BLUE MYSTIC Street drug 2C-T-7, also called Triptasy or 7-Up (See TRYPTAMINE).

BLUE NITRO Common GBL product (GHB analog) disguised as a dietary supplement.

BLUES Amytal Sodium capsule.

BLUE STAR A type of Morning Glory plant. The seeds can cause hallucinations similar to that of LSD.

BLUE VELVET Tincture of Opium added to powdered Tripelennamine, made into a solution and injected for a very intense high.

BLUNT Hollowed out cigar filled with marijuana.

BO Street gang term for Marijuana.

BOAT 1,000 MDMA pills; also called a bucket in some regions.

BODY CARRIER Drug smuggler who carries the contraband in their clothes or on their body.

BODY PACKER Drug smuggler who swallows the contraband which is usually wrapped in balloons or condoms. Later it is retrieved after defecation (see MULE).

BOGART Not sharing any drug.

BOMBED Excessive drug intoxication.

BOLIVIAN

a. Cocaine of the purest form
b. Country of origin

BOLSA Spanish word for bag. Usually refers to Heroin.

BOLT Amyl Nitrite.

BONG Marijuana smoking pipe that is usually glass with a cooling chamber that is filled with water or wine.

BOWL

a. Marijuana pipe
b. A degree measurement of Marijuana

BOTTLE 100 pills.

BOY Heroin.

BOWL PARTY See PHARMING, TRAIL MIX.

BRICK A quantity of Marijuana compressed into the shape of a brick that usually weighs a kilogram (2.2 lbs.).

BRING DOWN

a. To precipitate a "crash" from the excessive agitation produced by stimulants, via the ingestion of a CNS depressant
b. To help reduce highly adverse effects produced in some h hallucinogen users via talk, reassurance, and sometimes minor tranquilizers

BRING IT UP To bulge a vein prior to injection.

BRODY, TO THROW A To feign illness or withdraw in an attempt to obtain a narcotic prescription from a sympathetic physician.

BROTHER Heroin.

BROWN STUFF Mexican Brown Powdered Heroin.

BROWNIES Regular fudge brownies mixed with Marijuana.

BRUXISM Teeth grinding and jaw locking commonly caused by drugs such as MDMA and methamphetamine.

BUBBLES 4-methylmethcathinone (See MEPHEDRONE).

BUCKET 1,000 MDMA pills in some regions; more commonly called a boat (See BOAT).

BUD The blossom at the top of the Marijuana plant that contains the highest level of THC which is the active component of the plant.

BUDDHA STICK Potent Asian Marijuana which is wrapped around bamboo sticks for shipping.

BUFF/BUFFED

a. To dilute a drug
b. Muscular in appearance from use of steroids and/or exercise

BUG Itching sensation, due to cocaine overdose.

BUGGER Black Tar Heroin.

BULLET

a. Bullet-shaped plastic tube used for snorting drugs in the powdered form
b. One year jail term

BUMMED/BUMMER

a. Bad trip
b. A bad experience not necessarily drug related

BUMP (AKA: LINE)

a. Refers to a line, a bump or pile of cocaine, meth, MDMA or ketamine powder to be snorted, usually 0.2 grams per line
b. Internet jargon on message boards for agreeing with the last person/message

BUM TRIP A bad hallucinogenic drug experience.

BUNK Low grade drug. Often the adulterant is solo and being represented as the drug.

BURN Substances used to dilute potency of drug such as lidocaine, procaine, nicotinamide, or ephedrine.

BURNED Cheated by a drug dealer.

BURNED OUT In a state of brain or chronic behavior impairment resulting from chronic heavy drug use.

BUSH Marijuana.

BUSINESSMAN'S LUNCH DMT, a hallucinogen with potent effects lasting 30–60 minutes.

BUST An arrest by authorities and confiscation of drugs.

BUTTON The top middle flower area of the Peyote Cactus (Hemispheric Tabercculous). A hard, round object, slightly larger than a golf ball, containing the active ingredient of the plant, Mescaline, a hallucinogen.

BUTYL NITRATE A chemical abused by inhalation for the intense rush it provides; was sold over the counter in small vials as incense, cleaner, etc.; may still be diverted from legitimate chemical use.

BUY A drug purchase.

BUZZ A drug high.

BZP In medical notes may refer to benzodiazepine but in the street refers to BENZYLPIPERAZINE, another drug abused by MDMA users for the related effects (See also TFMPP or MOLLY).

C Cocaine.

C&H Cocaine and Heroin.

CABALLO Spanish word for Heroin.

CACTUS Peyote Cactus.

CADET First time drug user.

CALIFORNIA SUNSHINE LSD produced and sold on the West Coast.

CAMEL Drug smuggler or drug carrier.

CAN One ounce quantity of Marijuana.

CANDY Cocaine or MDMA.

CANDY FLIP Refers to the polydrug "flip" of taking both MDMA and LSD; users are encouraged to take the LSD about three hours before taking Ecstasy (See FLIP).

CANDY MAN Drug dealer or drug supplier.

CANDY RAVER Rave attendee who dresses in infantile garb, wears bead/candy necklaces and pacifiers and takes the drug MDMA (Ecstasy) (See RAVE).

CAP

a. Powdered drug in capsule form
b. GHB users typically dose in caps, measured by water bottle caps, for example, which is about 6–7ml

CAP-UP To put powdered drugs into capsules.

CARGA Spanish word for Heroin.

CARRIER Drug smuggler or transporter.

CARTWHEELS White Amphetamine tablets.

CAT FOOD 4-methylmethcathinone (See MEPHEDRONE).

CAT

a. Heroin
b. A synthetic designer drug, methcathinone, a stimulant with no medical application

CAT VALIUM The drug ketamine, primarily used as a small animal anesthetic but also has use in pediatrics and as a battlefield anesthetic.

CATHINONE and CATHINE The leaves of the Khat (or catha edulis) plant common to locations such as Somolia, often chewed for the stimulant effect; when fresh, the leaves contain cathinone, a Schedule I substance, but once dried, the substance deteriorates to the weaker version, cathine, which is on Schedule IV.

CCC Refers to the brand "Coricidin Cough & Cold" tablets containing dextromethorphan (DXM), widely abused by teens who take from 10 to 45 pills at a time (See also RED DEVILS, TRIPLE C, THE MATRIX, DXM).

CECIL/CEC Cocaine.

CHANNEL Vein used for injecting drugs.

CENT One dollar.

CHAPAPOTE Spanish word for Mexican Tar Heroin.

CHARAS Hindu for Marijuana.

CHARGE The first effect of a drug high.

CHARLIE Cocaine.

CHASING THE DRAGON Heating Heroin or Opium on a piece of foil and inhaling the smoke.

CHEESE "Starter heroin" made by mixing ground up Tylenol PM© or Benadryl© (both contain diphenhydramine, an antihistamine with sedating properties) tablets with up to approximately 8 percent of heroin to introduce teens to taking heroin. Mostly in the Dallas, Texas, area (also seen as Chees, Cheez, Chez, Chz, Queso, Keso, Kso in text and email messages).

CHINA WHITE

a. Southeastern Asian Heroin
b. The synthetic opiate Alpha-Methylfentanyl.

CHIPPER/TO CHIP

a. An occasional drug user
b. To inject just under the skin

CHIPPING Taking narcotic analgesics on an occasional or irregular basis, not sufficiently often enough to become physically dependent.

CHIVA Spanish word for Heroin.

CHOKING GAME A method of self-asphyxiation by cutting off the supply of oxygen/blood flow to the brain by pressing the thumbs against the carotid artery for the high or rush it gives and causing the person to pass out briefly, fall limp and thus release the flow of blood; this game has been around for years but has reached higher risk levels by involving others as the choker and utilizing belts or other props, increasing the risk that airflow or blood flow would be withheld too long, causing brain damage or death; participants are often young teens.

CHOPPING To dilute or adulterate a drug.

CHRISTMAS TREES The prescription drug Tuinal.

CHRONIC High grade marijuana.

CIRCLES Rohypnol.

CLEAN Drug free.

CLENBUTEROL Abused by some bodybuilders/athletes for alleged fat burning, stimulant and muscle enhancing effects, despite negative side effects.

CLUB DRUGS Common term for a variety of drugs used in rave and nightclub scene, loosely including MDMA (Ecstasy), LSD, ketamine, GHB, meth, marijuana and other hallucinogens.

CLUCK HEAD Street gang term for Cocaine addict.

COASTING The euphoric high just after taking a drug, usually associated with Heroin.

COAST TO COASTS Amphetamine tablets.

COCAINE BLUES Depression from discontinuing use of cocaine.

COKE Cocaine.

COKE BUGS The sensation of bugs crawling under or on the user's skin associated with a Cocaine overdose.

COKE HEAD A Cocaine user.

COKE SPOON A small metal spoon used for snorting (inhaling) Cocaine.

COKED OUT Excessive use of cocaine to point of incoherence.

COKED UP Label for erratic behavior due to excessive use of cocaine.

COLA Cocaine.

COLD TURKEY Abrupt withdrawal from long term drug abuse.

COLUM Street gang term used for Colombian Marijuana.

COME DOWN The gradual wearing-off of the effects of drugs.

COME-ON The first feeling after taking a drug.

COMMERCIAL Street gang term used for Marijuana.

CONNECT/CONNECTION Drug dealer or supplier.

CONTACT HIGH Mild euphoria occurring in non-smokers and believed by them to be the result of inhalation of the Marijuana fumes produced by smokers.

COOK To prepare or heat a drug into liquid form in preparation for injection.

COOKED High on drugs.

COOKER

a. The container in which drugs are heated for injection. For example: Spoons, bottle caps, bottom half of a soft drink or beer can, etc.
b. One who manufactures drugs in a lab

COOKIE Chunk of rock cocaine.

COOKING COTTONS When a Heroin addict can not get Heroin, he will use the old cotton.

COP To purchase drugs.

CO-PILOT An individual knowledgeable about the effects of hallucinogens, particularly in the case of LSD The Co-Pilot provides reassurance and reality for the novice user (See BABYSITTER).

CORINE Cocaine.

COTTON A small amount of cotton used to filter impurities from dissolved Heroin as it is drawn into the hypodermic.

COTTON, ASKING FOR Refers to an impoverished heroin addict to afford a "buy" scrounging the cotton used as a filter by other addicts that a very weak heroin solution can be made.

COTTON FEVER During the process of injecting, a small piece of cotton is used as a filter when the drug, usually Heroin, is drawn up into the syringe. Occasionally a fiber of cotton is drawn up into the syringe and is injected causing the user to become extremely ill.

COTTON MOUTH Dry mouth caused by ingestion of certain drugs.

COURIER Drug smuggler or transporter.

CRACK Cocaine Hydrochloride (powder) that has been processed into a pure solid form for smoking.

CRACK HOUSE A structure where Crack (Freebased Cocaine) is sold.

CRACKER A device used to "crack open" small nitrous oxide cartridges and divert the gas into a balloon for huffing (See NITROUS OXIDE or WHIPPETS).

CRANK Methamphetamine.

CRANKSTER User of Methamphetamine.

CRANK BUGS The sensation of bugs crawling on or under the user's skin associated with a Methamphetamine overdose.

CRAP

a. Heroin
b. Low quality drug

CRASH To abruptly stop using a drug.

CRATE A large quantity of pills, usually 50,000.

CRATER A deep flesh indentation at a particular site which has been subjected to repeated intravenous injections.

CRINK Methamphetamine.

CROKE To use Cocaine and Methamphetamine together.

CROSS-TOPS Benzedrine tablets, so named for the crossed lines on one side of the pill as a result of the pill press mold.

CRYSTAL Methamphetamine.

CUBE A sugar cube containing LSD.

CUT To adulterate or dilute drugs.

CYCLING Using different types of steroids one after another, but not at the same time. Example: Use a particular type of steroid for a period of time then use a different type of steroid to gain the maximum effect and reduce side effects.

D LSD.

D & G MDMA pills with the logo D&G for clothing designers Dolce & Gabanna, one of many business logos used on the illicit pills.

DANCE Refers to the drug carisoprodol (tradename Soma).

DANCING Mixing the effects of carisoprodol (Soma) with alcohol.

DATE RAPE DRUG (RAPE DRUG) Any drug used to render someone unable to give or withhold consent to sexual activity, such as CNS depressants or hallucinogens (See DFSA).

DATURA The genus of plants commonly called jimson weed, angel's trumpet, moonflower, devil's weed; leaves, seeds and roots contain atropine, scopolamine and hyoscyamine, three toxic alkaloids; abuse by smoking or making tea to hallucinate can be fatal.

DAVA Heroin.

DAZZLE The depressant drug midazolam (tradename Versed) which is from the family of benzodiazepines.

DEAD PRESIDENTS Street gang term for money.

DEAL/DEALER To sell drugs/One who sells drugs.

DEATH Refers to the drugs PMA and PMMA, similar to MDMA but more intense in effects and have a greater risk of death.

DESIGNATED SITTER Someone who babysits others who are tripping on hallucinogens.

DESIGNER DRUG Drugs designed by chemists as similar to the chemistry and property of other drugs, often to try to sidestep the law if the primary drug is already illegal. Also loosely used interchangeably by some with the term Club Drugs (See ANALOG).

DEVIL DUST PCP.

DEXIES The prescription stimulant drug Dexedrine.

DFSA or DRUG FACILITATED SEXUAL ASSAULT The use of drugs to render a person unable to give or withhold consent to have sex (See DATE RAPE DRUG).

DIAMONDS Amphetamine tablets.

DILLIES Dilaudid (Hydromorphine).

DIME Ten dollars.

DIME BAG Ten dollars worth of a drug.

DIRTY

a. To possess drugs
b. To give a positive body fluid test

DIRTY PEE Positive urine test.

DITCH WEED Low quality Marijuana.

D.M.T. The synthetic hallucinogen Dimethyltryptamine, also called "Business-man's lunch because the effects last less than an hour.

DO A LINE To snort (inhale) a "line" of a drug in powder form.

DOING CAPS Taking GHB by the capful.

DO UP To inject.

D.O.A. Dead on arrival.

DOB 2,5 dimethyoxy-4-bromoamphetamine, potent hallucinogen, one of many that may be encountered as a substitute for MDMA.

DOLLAR One hundred dollars worth of a drug.

DOLLY Dolophine (Methadone).

DOOBIE Marijuana cigarette (See JOINT).

DOORS & FOURS Taking the prescription drugs Doriden and Tylenol with Codeine #4 together. The effects are similar to that of Heroin.

DOPE General term for drugs.

DOPE FIEND Drug user.

DOPER Drug user.

DOSE

a. The amount of a drug taken
b. The amount of Methadone, a synthetic narcotic used to treat Heroin addiction, that is taken

DOSING Taking drugs.

DOT A dose of LSD so small it is hard to see.

DOUBLE STACK An MDMA (Ecstasy) pill that is double thick in size and dosage; also a nickname for the deadly drug PMA that is similar to MDMA but more severe.

DOWNER Barbiturates or tranquilizers.

DOWN, GET DOWN Inject a drug.

DRAGGED A mild anxiety and fatigue state following Marijuana intoxication.

DREAMERS Narcotic analgesic drugs.

DRIVERS The prescription drug Benzedrine, however, it is no longer manufactured (See BENNIES and BENZ).

DRONE 4-methylmethcathinone (See MEPHEDRONE).

DROP To take a drug orally.

DROP A TAB To take LSD orally.

DROP A DIME To inform on someone.

DROPPER Hypodermic syringe.

DRUGGIE Drug user.

DRY
a. To be drug free
b. When the supply of drugs are low or gone

DRY OUT To abstain from drugs or alcohol after a prolonged use, to the point of substantial or complete loss of tolerance.

DRY UP When drugs, usually narcotics, are not available.

DUCKETS Street gang term for money.

DUST
a. A drug in powder form
b. Cocaine
c. PCP (Phencyclidine)

DUST OFF A commercial air cleaner for computers, etc., that is being abused as an inhalant (See DUSTING).

DUSTED Under the influence of PCP.

DUSTER PCP USER.

DUSTING
a. Combining marijuana and heroin and rolling it in a form to be smoked
b. Inhaling the spray product DUST OFF

DXM The cough suppressant dextromethorphan, commonly abused especially by teens; taken in quantities from 300 to 900 milligrams to achieve high and/or hallucinations.

DYNO High quality drug.

EASY LAY The drug gamma hydroxybutyrate, GHB.

EAT To swallow drugs rather than be caught with them.

ECHOES LSD flashbacks.

ECSTACY Refers to ephedrine and herbal products seeking to resemble the drug MDMA in terms of stimulating effects. Note the spelling difference from the drug MDMA's nickname ECSTASY.

E/ECSTASY The synthetic drug MDMA (3,4-Methylenedioxy-N-Methylamphetamine); See also XTC or X.

EIGHT BALL 1/8 ounce of a drug.

EIGHTH 1/8 of an ounce or a gram.

ELEPHANT PCP (Phencyclidine).

ELEPHANT FLIP The polydrug flip of PCP and MDMA.

ELEVEN-FIVE-FIFTY Under the influence of a controlled substance, California Health & Safety Code section violation (11550 H&S).

EMBALMING FLUID An old nickname for PCP but current use also involves the actual abuse of embalming fluid, which contains formaldehyde and gives a similar bizarre behavior state but without the analgesic effect of pain blocking (see PCP, FRY CIGARETTES, ILLY).

EMERALD TRIANGLE The California counties of Mendocino, Humbolt, and Trinity. This area is known for growing the high grade Sinsemilla Marijuana.

EQUIPMENT Drug paraphernalia.

E-PRESSED Slang for the after effects of MDMA (Ecstasy) depression due to the draining of serotonin levels by this drug.

E PUDDLE Refers to MDMA (Ecstasy) abusers as they often pile up together due to fatigue and/or the general effects of the drug; also called a Cuddle Puddle.

EQUIPOISE A veterinary steroid product, commonly diverted and abused by steroid users, that contains boldenone undecylenate.

E-TARD Someone on MDMA, Ecstasy.

E-TARDATION The "dumbing down" effects of abusing the drug MDMA.

EUPHORIA or U4EUH Hallucinogen 4-methylaminorex.

EVERCLEAR
a. 190 proof grain alcohol
b. Slang for gamma hydroxybutyrate (GHB)

EYE CANDY Refers to flashing lights and toys that captivate people who are on the drug MDMA.

EYE OPENER The first Heroin injection of the day.

FACTORY A location where illicit drugs are produced for street sale.

FANTASIA Dimethyltryptamine or DMT.

FANTASY Gamma hydroxybutyrate (GHB) nickname common in Australia where is has been widely abused by bodybuilders and raver/club attendees.

FENTANYL A powerful anesthetic drug. Fentanyl may be diverted from hospitals for use. Analogs of fentanyl are usually manufactured illegally in clandestine drug labs.

FINGER An amount of Marijuana or Hashish.

FIRE A LINE To snort (inhale) an amount of a powdered drug.

FIRE UP To light and smoke a Cocaine or Methamphetamine pipe.

FIRE WATER A GBL product sold as a dietary supplement but now illegal as a GHB analog.

FIRED UP A drug high usually associated with Cocaine or Methamphetamine.

FIT Paraphernalia for injecting drugs.

FIVE CENTS Five dollars worth of a drug.

FIX To inject a drug.

FLAKE Cocaine.

FLAKY Acting crazy.

FLASH/FLASHING The first effect of a drug.

FLASHBACK A reoccurrence of a drug usually associated with LSD or PCP. The drug is stored in the fat cells and may reenter the body months or even years after the last ingestion.

FLASH POWDER Methamphetamine.

FLATLINERS Street drug 4-methylthioamphetamine (4-MTA), also called Golden Eagle.

FLIP Polydrug abuse referring to taking, or "flipping" MDMA with other drugs for variation of effects (See CANDY FLIP, HIPPIE FLIP, ELEPHANT FLIP, SEXTASY, LUCKY FLIP).

FLIP OUT To experience a severe psychological reaction to a drug.

FLOATING Intoxicated.

FLOWER OF PARADISE Refers to khat, a plant often abused in Ethiopian, Somali and Yemeni communities. (See "Cathinone" in stimulant section).

FLUFFING Chopping up Cocaine with a razor blade into a fine powder. It is then strained through mesh to increase its volume.

FLYING SAUCER Trade name for Morning Glory seeds.

FOILING Placing a drug, usually Heroin, on a piece of tin foil, then heating it up and inhaling the smoke.

FOURS 60 mg. Codeine tablets stamped with the number 4.

FOXY OR FOXY METHOXY Street drug 5-methoxy-N,N-diisopropyltryptamine (5-MEO-DIPT), usually seen in pills with a spider or alien imprint.

FREAK One who chronically uses large amounts of a specific drug.

FREEBASE or FREEBASING A style of smoking rock cocaine.

FREEZE.

a. Unavailability of drugs
b. Numbness caused by using cocaine

FRIED

a. Drug high
b. Close to an overdose

FRONT

a. To acquire drugs when payment is to be made by a reliable third party known to the seller
b. To purchase drugs on a short term credit

FRUIT SALAD A reckless combination of drugs.

FRY CIGARETTES or FRY STICKS Regular cigarettes or marijuana cigarettes dipped in PCP and/or embalming fluid (See PCP, EMBALMING FLUID & WETS).

GANJA Hindu for Marijuana. Also used in the Jamaican culture.

GAP To yawn (one of the earliest symptoms of heroin withdrawal).

GARBAGE Low grade drugs.

GBL Gamma butyrolactone, primary ingredient for GHB and an active analog that turns rapidly into GHB in the human body. GBL is a degreasing solvent (See ANALOG).

GEE Gasket between needle and syringe.

GEED UP or JEED UP or G'D UP High on gamma hydroxybutyrate (GHB).

GEEZE To inject a drug.

GET DOWN To use drugs, but is usually associated with Heroin.

GET OFF The first effects of a drug.

GHB Gamma hydroxybutyric acid (like liquid ecstasy). Illegal in U.S. except for limited prescription use under the tradename Xyrem (federal Schedule III drug). If Xyrem is diverted for abuse, it is treated as a Schedule I drug, the same as illicit GHB.

GINA Common gym name for gamma hydroxybutyrate (GHB).

GIRL Cocaine.

GLASS Pure, solid, smokable form of Crystal Methamphetamine (See ICE).

GOD'S MEDICINE Morphine.

GO/GO FAST Outdated term for stimulant drugs, usually associated with Amphetamines.

GOLD A particularly potent form of Marijuana grown in the Acapulco area (See ACAPULCO GOLD and GOLD LEAF).

GOLD DUST Cocaine.

GOLDEN CRESCENT The Opium producing area of Southwest Asia (Iran, Pakistan, and Afghanistan).

GOLDEN TRIANGLE The Opium producing area of Southeast Asia (Burma, Laos, and Thailand).

GOLD LEAF A particularly potent form of Marijuana grown in the Acapulco area (See ACAPULCO GOLD and GOLD).

GOMA Spanish word for Mexican Tar Heroin.

GOODS Refers to narcotics.

GOOFBALLS Barbiturates.

GRAM Common amount or measurement of a drug.

GRASS Marijuana.

GRAVEL Crack Cocaine.

GRIFA Spanish word for Marijuana.

GYM CANDY Street term for anabolic steroid.

GUIDE A baby sitter for an abuser of hallucinogenic drugs during an experience.

GUN Injection paraphernalia for Heroin.

HABIT Drug addiction.

HALF 1/2 gram or 1/2 ounce of a drug.

HALLUCINOGEN Also referred to as psychedelic drugs, these substances may be either natural or synthetic and produce various intensities of hallucinations (perceptual changes involving sound, sight, sense of touch or smell, etc.).

HAMMER COMING DOWN The rapid and dramatic transition from a normal feeling state to that which results from a full impact of a drug. Usually in reference to the effects of a drug intravenously administered.

HARD DRUGS Narcotic analgesics. Also used to cover any drug which is controlled by a federal narcotic statutes, such as cannabis or cocaine.

HANYAK Solid, smokable Methamphetamine.

HAPPY DRUG OR HAPPY PILL The drug MDMA.

HAPPY DUST Cocaine.

HARD STUFF Heroin.

HASH The isolated active ingredient of the Marijuana plant, THC; Hash comes in solid and oil form.

HAY Marijuana.

HEAD A heavy regular user of a drug. Reference is often made to a specific drug, such as "Acid Head".

HEAD SHOP A store that sells drug paraphernalia and other related drug items.

HEARTS Dexedrine tablets.

HEAVENLY BLUE Strain of blue Morning Glory seeds which can be abused by sucking large quantities or making tea from them. Legend is that the blue ones are more potent.

HEAVES Violent vomiting occurring during drug withdrawal.

HEMP Marijuana.

HERB Marijuana.

HIERBA Street name (Spanish) for marijuana.

HIGH Drug induced euphoria.

HIPPIE or HIPPY FLIP Polydrug flip of MDMA and magic mushrooms.

HIT

a. Injection of drugs
b. A puff of a Marijuana Cigarette

HIT UP
a. To inject a drug
b. To borrow or attempt to borrow

HOG PCP (Phencyclidine).

HOLDING To possess drugs.

HONEY OIL Purified Hashish Oil containing the highest concentration of THC.

HOOKA Marijuana smoking pipe or bong (See BONG).

HOOKED Addicted to drugs.

HORN To snort (inhale) drugs in powder form.

HORSE Heroin.

HOT SHOT A very pure dose of Heroin which can result in death.

HOUSEWIFE'S DISEASE Dependence on tranquilizers.

HUBBA Cocaine Freebase.

HUFFER A person who uses inhalants such as glue, paint thinner, petroleum products, etc.

HUFFING The act of using inhalants.

HUG DRUG MDMA (Ecstasy).

HUNTING Desperately seeking drugs prior to the onset of withdrawal.

HUSTLING Addicts attempts to obtain enough money to purchase more drugs.

HYPE Heroin addict.

ICE Pure, solid, smokable form of Crystal Methamphetamine (See GLASS). Also refers to 4-methylaminorex, which is often called Euphoria or U4EUH.

ILLY CIGARETTE or ILLIES Regular cigarettes or marijuana cigarettes dipped in PCP and/or embalming fluid (See EMBALMING FLUID, WETS, FRYS).

J Marijuana.

JAB To inject.

JACKING OFF THE NEEDLE After putting the needle into the vein, some users pull the needle in and out of the wound to be sure the needle is still in the vein. This is usually associated with Heroin use.

JAG State of being under influence of solvents.

JANE Marijuana.

JAR 100 or 1000 pills, also known as jug.

JELLY Cocaine.

JENKEM Fecal matter & urine are fermented; the gas is captured in a balloon and then inhaled for a brief high. Allegedly done in poverty areas in some countries. Not likely widely practiced anywhere.

JET FUEL PCP.

JIB Street name for gamma hydroxybutyrate (GHB).

JIM JONES Street gang term for Marijuana cigarette laced with Cocaine and dipped in PCP.

JIMSON WEED A hallucinogenic weed from the Datura genus (See DATURA).

JOINT Marijuana cigarette.

JOLT The first effects of a drug.

JONES A drug habit.

JOY POP Irregular use of narcotics.

JONESING Needing a drug fix.

JOY POPPING To inject just under the skin usually associated with Heroin use.

JUG 1,000 pills.

JUICE

a. Cheap wine
b. More recently, liquid preparations of narcotic analgesic cough suppressants
c. PCP (Phencyclidine)
d. Steroids
e. GHB

JUNK Diluted Heroin.

JUNKIE Drug addict.

JUNK WEED Low grade Marijuana.

K Kilogram (2.2 pounds).

K or KET Ketamine.

K2 Herbal mixtures combined with synthetic cannabinoids or cannabinoid-mimicking compounds such as HU-210 and JWH-018 have been surfacing worldwide in a variety of products also referred to by various names, including Spice, Genie, Skunk and Sense. (See SPICE).

KAKSONJAE Pure, solid, smokable form of Crystal Methamphetamine.

KAVA KAVA Sold as a dietary supplement, kava is a root common to the South Pacific, containing piper methysticum, that is a mild depressant.

KETAMINE Animal tranquilizer for small animals, especially cats, that is also used on a limited basis in humans (in pediatrics and as a war zone anesthetic).

K-HOLE A ketamine induced out of body and/or comatose state.

KIBBLES & BITS Street gang term for small pieces of freebase cocaine.

KEG 50,000 pills.

KEESTER PLANT Drugs which are hidden in the rectum.

KGB (KILLER GREEN BUD) Marijuana.

KHAT A plant common to areas like Somolia; leaves are chewed for stimulant effect of cathinone (when leaves are fresh) or cathine (once dried) (See CATHINONE and CATHINE).

KICK Stop using drugs.

KILLER JOINT or KILLER WEED

a. Marijuana cigarette laced with PCP
b. Very potent Marijuana

KILO Kilogram (2.2 pounds).

KING'S HABIT The use of Cocaine.

KIT Paraphernalia for injecting drugs.

KITTY FLIP The polydrug abuse of using MDMA and ketamine together; abusers are advised to take the MDMA 15 minutes before taking the ketamine (See FLIP).

KJ PCP-saturated menthol cigarette (See KOOL JOINT).

KNOCKOUT DRUGS Liquid Chloral Hydrate or other drug, typically used with alcohol, to facilitate rape or robbery; Additional Comments: Despite the terminology, not all drugs used to facilitate rape result in being unconscious. Amnesia is the primary effect for many of them and unconsciousness may or may not occur at some point.

KONA GOLD High grade Hawaiian Marijuana.

KOOL JOINT Menthol cigarette laced with PCP (See KJ).

KRATOM Unregulated recreational herbal plant increasingly being used for stimulating effects in low doses or opiate, sedating effects in higher doses.

KRYSTAL Crystal Methamphetamine.

L LSD.

LACE To add a drug to another substance. Example: To spray PCP on Marijuana for smoking.

LACTONE Gammabutyrolactone (GBL), which is the primary ingredient in GHB but also an active analog; if consumed, GBL converts rapidly in the body to GHB.

LADY Cocaine.

LAUGHING GAS Nitrous oxide, used legitimately by dentists mixed with controlled level of oxygen but abused by huffing for the brief high that may result in brief unconsciousness (See NITROUS OXIDE).

L.A. TURNAROUNDS Amphetamines.

L.B. 1 pound of a drug.

LEAF Marijuana.

LEAPERS Amphetamines.

LEB Lebanese Hashish.

LIBS The prescription drug Librium.

LID An ounce of marijuana.

LIGHT UP To smoke marijuana.

LINE An amount of powdered drugs such as cocaine, meth, MDMA or ketamine that is combed (with a credit card or razor) into thin lines (on a mirror or glass or smooth surface) for snorting (with a straw or rolled up paper currency, etc.) (See BUMP).

LIQUID XTC or LIQUID X or LIQUID ECSTASY Refers to the drug GHB which is most commonly found in liquid state; does not refer to MDMA (Ecstasy) though some abusers have accidentally taken it believing it is a liquid version of MDMA.

LOADED Under the influence of a drug.

LOADS Tylenol® w/ Codeine® #4 and Doriden®

LOCO WEED Marijuana.

LOVE DRUGS MDA, Methqualone.

LOVE FLIP Polydrug abuse of MDMA and Mescaline.

LOVELY PCP.

LSA d-lysergic acid amide is a precursor chemical to LSD and can be derived by sucking on morning glory seeds or drinking tea made from the seeds.

LSD The synthetic hallucinogen D-Lysergic Acid Diethylamide.

LUCKY FLIP Polydrug abuse of MDMA and Lucky 7 (2-CT-7).

LUCKY 7 Street drug 2C-T-7, also called Triptasy, T7, 7-UP and Blue Mystic (See TRYPTAMINE).

LUDES Quaaludes (No longer manufactured).

M

a. Marijuana
b. Morphine

M&M'S MDMA (3,4-Methylenedioxyl-N-Methylamphetamine).

MAGIC DUST PCP.

MAGIC MUSHROOM Refers to Psilocybin.

MAKE A BUY Purchase drugs.

MAINLINE To inject intravenously.

MAN Drug dealer or drug connection.

MANICURE The removal of unusable parts of the Marijuana plant such as stocks, stems, seeds, etc.

MANNITOL Cutter for cocaine.

MAPS The Multidisciplinary Association for Psychedelic Studies is a nonprofit group that promotes research of all psychedelic drugs and promotes legalization.

MARKS Puncture wounds or holes left from needle injection.

MARKED UP Displaying puncture wounds from needle injections.

MARY JANE Marijuana.

MATCHBOX 1/2 ounce of marijuana.

MAUI WOWIE High grade Marijuana from Hawaii.

MDA Mellow Drug of America. The synthetic hallucinogen drug 3,4-Methylenedioxyamphetamine.

MDMA 3,4-Methylenedioxy-N-Methylamphetamine is a synthetic hallucinogen with stimulant qualities.

MEOW-MEOW 4-methylmethcathinone (See MEPHEDRONE).

MEPHEDRONE Marketed on the Internet as a "plant food," mephedrone is 4-methylmethcathinone (4-MMC). It is a stimulant with some psychotropic effects much like MDMA (Ecstasy). It is also known as drone, bubble or bubbles, meow meow, MM-Cat, M-Cat, cat food, and Sunshine.

MEQUIN Methaqualone.

MERCK Pharmaceutical Cocaine.

MERSH Low grade Marijuana.

MESC Mescaline.

METH Methamphetamine.

METH MOUTH Deterioration of the teeth from exposure to the chemicals involved in methamphetamine and drug's effect of causing mouth dryness.

METHADONE Methadone is most commonly known for use in heroin addiction treatment; it is also a pain medication being more widely prescribed, resulting in increased abuse and deaths.

METHCATHINONE A street drug stimulant related to meth and often called CAT.

METH HEAD User of methamphetamine.

MEXICAN BROWN Mexican brown heroin.

MEXICAN MUD Mexican black tar heroin.

MICKEY FINN The combination of the prescription drug Chloral Hydrate and Alcohol.

MICRO DOTS LSD on very small tablets.

MIERA Spanish word for Heroin.

MIKE Microgram.

MILK From milk sugar. Crystals of lactose frequently used in diluting Heroin.

MIND-BLOWING Referring to a drug that produces extraordinarily powerful reaction. Usually a favorable experience.

MINI BEANS Small Benzedrine tablets.

MISS EMMA Morphine.

MITSUBISHI MDMA pill with the Mitsubishi corporate logo imprinted; pill may be round, triangular or pentagon shaped; a very common logo.

MJ Marijuana.

MMDA 3-Methoxy-4, 5 Methylenedioxyamphetamine which is a psychedelic Amphetamine.

MOLLY The drug TFMPP or 1-(3-Trifluoromethylphenyl) piperazine is referred to as Molly and is typically in capsule form; same clientele as MDMA and similar effects.

MONKEY The state of being in withdrawal from Heroin.

MOTA Spanish word for Marijuana.

MOUTH HABIT Oral drug use.

MPPP One of the numerous, so called "Designer Drugs" similar to MPTP. Gives Heroin-like effects and can be made to look like White Heroin.

MPTP Made from MPPP and is another "Designer Drug" with effects like White Heroin.

MSM Methyl sulfone or methylsulfoylmethane is a naturally occurring organic sulfur compound, sold as a dietary supplement; also used as a cutting agent for meth; extends quantity and gives a whiter product.

MUD Mexican black tar heroin.

MULE A drug smuggler who actually carries the drugs.

MUNCHIES Constant snacking associated with Marijuana intoxication.

MUSCLING Injecting drugs into the muscle and is most commonly associated with steroids.

NAIL Hypodermic needle.

NARC

a. A narcotics officer
b. An informer
c. To inform on someone, "To narc someone off"

NEBBIES The prescription drug Nembutal.

NEEDLE FREAK One who injects drugs into the vein or skin.

NEEDLE MAN An addict.

NEXUS The drug 2-(4-Bromo-2,5-dimethoxy-phenyl)-ethylamine, also called 2C-B or Bromo.

NEXUS FLIPPING Taking MDMA and Nexus (See FLIP).

NICKEL Five dollars.

NICKEL BAG Five dollars worth of a drug.

NINETEEN A term for speed. The nineteenth letter of the alphabet is "S".

NOD Being under the influence of Heroin. A relaxed state similar to sleep.

NOSE CANDY Cocaine.

NOX Abusing nitrous oxide while on MDMA.

NOZ Reference to nitrous oxide.

N2O Nitrous oxide, abused by inhaling, causing a very brief high and possible brief unconsciousness; not scheduled but some states have laws against possession with intent to inhale (gas, devices for inhaling, etc.) and for inhaling or being impaired to drive.

NUBAIN Brand name for the drug nalbuphine, an analgesic for moderate to severe pain; widely used by athletes, often resulting in abuse and addiction.

NUKING THE COKE During the Cocaine Freebasing process the Cocaine Hydrochloride is mixed with baking soda and water, then heated. The microwave is used to speed up the process. A coffee maker machine may also be used.

NUTMEG Cooking herb abused by some in high quantities (5–20 grams) for hallucinogenic effects; contains myristicin (also contained in mace).

O

a. Cocaine
b. Opium

O.D. Overdose, usually a very serious condition.

OCOTEA Ocotea Cymbarum, distilled from the bark of trees native to Brazil, Paraguay and Colombia and containing safrole, a key precursor for making MDMA; also called Oil of Octea and Brazilian sassafras oil.

OIL

a. Hashish in oil form
b. Methamphetamine in oil form

OLLA Cocaine.

ONE HITTER A drug that can only be diluted one time.

ONE & ONE Two lines of Cocaine, one for each nostril.

ON THE PIPE Street gang term for being addicted to Freebase Cocaine.

ORANGE CRUSH When the red pills of Coridicin® Cough & Cold medication are crushed it results in an orange powder that is then snorted for the high from the DXM it contains (See DXM or DEXTROMETHORPHAN).

OTC Over the counter. Refers to drugs that can be bought without a prescription.

OUTFIT Paraphernalia for injecting drugs.

OUT OF SIGHT

a. Extraordinary quality, wonderful
b. A fantastic experience

OVERAMPED An overdose usually associated with a stimulant drug (Cocaine or Methamphetamine).

OXY/OXYCOTTON OxyContin, brandname for the synthetic opiate oxycodone; widely abused for its powerful euphoria but also potentially deadly.

OZ/OZER One ounce.

PAKALOLO Hawaiian for Marijuana.

PANAMA GOLD High grade Panamanian Marijuana.

PANAMA RED High grade Panamanian Marijuana that has a red color to the leaves and a red fuzz on the under portion of the leaves.

PANIC

a. An acute state of fear precipitated by the onset of withdrawl and frantic action to acquire drugs
b. An abrupt drying up of heroin sources, affecting all local addicts

PAPERS

a. Marijuana rolling papers (Zig-Zag being the most common)
b. Blotter acid
c. A piece of paper folded like an envelope containing a small amount of a drug (See BINDLE)

PAPER ACID LSD.

PARACHUTE MDMA powder or crushed MDMA pills or coke powder may be wrapped in tissue and swallowed in the belief that letting the drug "parachute" down in that manner intensifies the effect.

PARTY BOWL/PARTY BONG A Marijuana pipe (See BONG).

PAREST Methaqualone.

PASTA/PASTE Raw coca extracted from the coca leaves to be refined into Cocaine Hydrochloride. The raw coca is often smoked by the local peasants because of its availability and inexpensive price.

PAYS & OWES Paperwork (may be elaborate bookkeeping or scraps of paper) showing buyers, sales and/or money amounts re drug distribution; may be in code.

PCP Phencyclidine.

P.D.R. Physician's Desk Reference. A book that contains all the pharmaceutical drugs. Used by doctors.

PCE N-Ethyl-1 -Phenycyclhexylamine. An analog or member of the PCP family of drugs.

PEACE WEED Marijuana laced with PCP.

PEAKING Reaching the highest point while under the influence of a drug.

PEARL Cocaine.

PEARLS Amyl Nitrite.

PEANUT BUTTER CRANK Low grade crude Methamphetamine.

PEDAZO Spanish word for Heroin.

PEP PILL Amphetamine.

PERCS The prescription drug Percodan.

PERICO Spanish word for Cocaine.

PERSIAN BROWN Raw, unprocessed Morphine sold on the streets as Heroin.

PERSIAN WHITE High grade Persian Heroin.

PERUVIAN FLAKE South American high grade Cocaine and refers to the shape of the Cocaine crystals.

PEYOTL American Indian name for the Peyote Cactus.

PEZ LSD-laced PEZ candies.

PHARMING The dangerous practice of mixing a variety of prescription and/or over-the-counter medications in a bowl at a party and grabbing a few without regard for dosage and drug interaction; also called TRAIL MIX.

PHENETHYLAMINES A class of chemical compounds that produce hallucinogenic effects and varying degrees of stimulation, best known being MDMA, MDA, MDEA, 2-CB.

PHENNIES The prescription drug Phenobarbital.

PIECE 1 ounce, or 1 pound, of a drug.

PILL FREAK User of any type of pills.

PILLOW

a. Methamphetamine
b. Package of 1,000 Amphetamine tablets
c. Methaqualone

PINNED Constricted pupils (the size of a pinhead) that result when under the influence of Heroin or other narcotics.

PIN/PINNER A very thin Marijuana cigarette.

PINK HEARTS

a. Prescription drug Preludin
b. Fake stimulants that can be ordered out of magazines and contain Caffeine and/or Ephedrine

PINK LADIES The prescription drug Darvon.

PINKS Seconal (named for the color of the capsule).

PIPERAZINE A veterinary animal wormer; variations of it are abused drugs (See BZP and TFMPP) with stimulant and somewhat MDMA-like properties.

PIPERIDINE Used to make PCP.

PLATEAUING Peaking out on a drug to the point where the user no longer feels the designated effects. Usually used to describe steroids.

PLUGGING The practice of rectal insertion of MDMA pills.

PLUR Raver term standing for Peace Love Unity and Respect.

POLVO Spanish word for Cocaine.

POP

a. To take a tablet orally
b. To inject subcutaneous

POPPERS Amyl and Butyl Nitrite, which is administered by crushing the small vile in which it is contained and immediately inhaling the vapors.

POPPING

a. To swallow a drug
b. To inject a drug under the skin, not directly into the vein

POT Marijuana.

POT HEAD Marijuana user.

POWDERED Under the influence of Cocaine.

P-2-P Phenyl-2-Propanone. A chemical used to make methamphetamine.

PRIMO Street gang term for a Marijuana cigarette laced with Cocaine.

PROCAINE Adulterant used to dilute the strength of cocaine or Mexican brown heroin; has pharmacological action of its own.

PROGESTEREX Fake drug touted in email over several years claiming that women are being drug raped and given Protesterex which will render them infertile. There is no such drug.

PROP Phenly-2-Propanone. A chemical used for manufacturing methamphetamine.

PSYCHEDELIC A drug that distorts visual, auditory, and tactil senses.

PUMPERS Street term for anabolic steroid.

PUNTA ROJA High grade Columbium Marijuana.

PURPLE HEARTS Phenobarbital (Luminal tablets).

PURPLE STICKY Brand name in head shops for Mexican salvia (See SALVIA DIVINORUM).

PUSHER Seller of drugs at the street level.

PYRAMIDS Brightly colored gelatin LSD on pieces of diffuser plastic (from fluorescent light fixtures, for example); may be peeled off of the plastic and cut into little strips like modern-day breath mint strips or the plastic may be perforated and then broken into square or rectangular pieces which are sucked on by the user.

Q'S Methaqualone.

QUARTER

a. 1/4 gram of a drug
b. 1/4 ounce of a drug
c. $25.00 worth of a drug

QUARTER PIECE 1/4 ounce of a certain drug.

RACK 2–5 capsules wrapped in tin foil.

RAGWEED Low grade Marijuana.

RAILS Lines of a powdered drug laid beside each other, on a mirror or a piece of glass, in preparation for snorting (inhaling).

RAINBOWS Tuinal (a combination of amobarbital and secobarbital) so called because of the bright red and blue capsules (See RED & BLUES).

RAT An informer.

RAVE PARTY All night electronic music party where most attendees use hallucinogens, especially MDMA (Ecstasy), and other drugs.

REDS/REDEVILS
a. Seconal
b. also refers to the red tablets containing DXM marketed as Coricidin Cough and Cold (See also ROBOTRIPPIN' and DXM)

RED & BLUES Tuinal. Bright red and blue capsules (See RAINBOWS).

REEFER A Marijuana cigarette.

REGISTER To find the vein when injecting.

RENEWTRIENENT A common GHB analog product disguised as a dietary supplement but illegal for human consumption; usually contains GBL.

RESIN The active ingredient of the Marijuana plant. THC (Delta-9-Tetrahydrocannabinol).

RIB Flunitrazepam, also known as Rohypnol.

RICIN A poisonous natural extract isolated from castor beans; falsely claimed to be used by meth traffickers to kill police officers, as per a fake alert that was being distributed via email in recent years.

RIG The paraphernalia used to inject drugs.

RIPPED
a. Exhausted after a several day amphetamine run
b. adversely affected by a drug
c. very muscular and lean

RIPPERS Amphetamines.

RIPPED OFF
a. Robbed
b. Cheated in a drug buy

ROACH The butt end of a Marijuana cigarette.

ROACH CLIP Any object used to hold the last bit of a burning Marijuana cigarette. An electrical alligator clip or surgical hemostat are commonly used.

ROACHED OUT High on flunitrazepam, trade name Rohypnol.

ROBOTRIPPIN' On DXM, named for Robitussin products that contain dextromethorphan, a cough suppressant that causes hallucinations in high doses.

ROCA Spanish word for Crack.

ROCK Freebased Cocaine Hydrochloride.

ROCK UP The process of converting Cocaine Hydrochloride to Cocaine base.

ROCKET FUEL PCP.

ROIDS General term for steroids.

ROID RAGE The uncontrollable, violent temperament displayed by some steroid users.

ROLL 10 pills sold in tin foil.

ROLLS MDMA pills.

ROLLING or ROLLIN' On MDMA (Ecstasy).

ROLLER PAPERS Cigarette rolling papers used to make Marijuana cigarettes.

ROMPUM Horse or large animal tranquilizer, analgesic, and muscle relaxant Xylazine; limited abuse by humans reported for euphoric effect.

ROOFIES/ROOPIES Flunitrazepam, tradename Rohypnol.

ROPE Marijuana.

RUBBY A skid row alcoholic who on occasion resorts to propyl (rubbing) alcohol.

RUDERALIS Russian Marijuana plant. It has a low percentage of THC, the active ingredient in Marijuana.

RUFFIES Flunitrazepam, tradename Rohypnol.

RUMMY Skid row alcoholic.

RUN A period of several consecutive days during which an individual uses Methamphetamines several times a day with little food or sleep.

RUNNER Drug smuggler or transporter.

RUSH An intense sensation which rapidly follows intravenous administration of such drugs as heroin, amphetamines or cocaine.

SAFROLE Key ingredient in MDMA; may appear as iso-safrole, bromo-safrole or chloro-safrole; a sassafras extract but is not present in sassafras candies sold legitimately. No legitimate chemical use in the USA.

SALTY WATER Nickname for GHB. Also referred to as WATER.

SALVIA DIVINORUM A hallucinogenic plant from the mint family that grows wild in some regions of Mexico and used by shamans there; active ingredient is salvinorin A, not scheduled as of 2005. More powerful than marijuana. Being touted on the Internet and in head shops (See PURPLE STICKY).

SATIVA Marijuana. Comes from the scientific name Cannabis Sativa.

SCHOOL BOY Codeine, so called because of the mildness of its effects when compared with the more potent narcotic analgesics.

SCOOP Common nickname for the drug GHB.

SCOPOLAMINE A Belladonna alkaloid (dispensed in transdermal patches) used to treat motion sickness by reducing nausea. Has been used in drug rape and robbery cases, causing amnesia and drowsiness. One of the three active ingredients in Jimson Weed (AKA: ZOMBIE DRUG).

SCORE To make a successful drug purchase.

SCRATCH Money.

SCREENS Round metal mesh screens placed in a smoking pipe to hold the drug in the bowl.

SCRIBE A person who writes false prescriptions.

SCRIPT Drug prescription.

SCRIPT WRITER Physician willing to write prescriptions for drugs.

SECOS Seconal.

SEND IT HOME To inject narcotic analgesics, cocaine or amphetamines intravenously.

SERVE Street gang term for selling drugs.

SES Sinsemilla Marijuana (Sinsemilla means without seeds).

SET A combination of the prescription drugs Doriden and Tylenol w/Codeine #4.

SET UP A situation in which undercover police officers entice a person to sell them drugs for the purpose of bringing about the person's arrest.

SEXTASY The "flip" of taking MDMA and Viagra together. The Viagra helps overcome the erectile dysfunction or blockage of orgasms that MDMA may cause.

SHABU Hawaiian word for the smokable form of Crystal Methamphetamine (See GLASS and ICE).

SHAKE The manicured leaves of a Marijuana plant.

SHAVE

a. To adulterate, dilute or shortweight a drug
b. Literally shave off minute quantities and thereby shortweight the buyer

SHEET ACID LSD on blotter paper (See BLOTTER ACID).

SHERMS A heavy-stock dark brown paper cigarette that is dipped into PCP and then smoked (Short for Shermans).

SHIT Low quality drugs. Usually refers to Heroin.

SHOOT-UP To inject intravenously.

SHOOTING GALLERY A place where heroin addicts congregate to inject.

SHORTCHANGED Having been sold drugs which are usually inferior in quality or purity.

SHOTGUNNING Using any available steroid.

SHOT IN THE ARM Although the general use of the term is now broader, it originally referred to an injection of narcotics, which is followed by a state of peacefulness, reverie and well-being.

SHROOMS The hallucinogenic Psilocybin Mushrooms.

SICKNESS The onset of withdrawal.

SINSEMILLA Spanish for "without seed." Marijuana from unfertilized female plants; it is a method of growing, not a variety of marijuana.

SIPPIN' SYRUP Drinking codeine cough syrup (promoted in a rap song).

SKAG Heroin.

SKIN POPPING Injecting subcutaneous.

SKITTLES or SKITTLING Refers to being on DXM (See DEXTROMETHORPHAN).

SKUNK WEED High grade Marijuana with a strong odor.

SLAB A large, flat piece of Freebased cocaine.

SLAMMING To inject. Usually refers to Heroin use.

SLEEPERS Sedative/hypnotic drugs such as barbiturates.

SLOW AND LOW Heroin users, when under the influence are said to be slow and low, in that they move slowly and speak in a low slow, slurred voice.

SMACK Heroin.

SMART DRINK Liquid concoctions containing various amino acids said to increase the intelligence of the user. Common at "rave" parties.

SMASHED Heavily intoxicated with alcohol or other drugs.

SMOKE Marijuana.

SMOKE HOUSE A structure where users go to smoke Freebase Cocaine. They "rent" the pipes which contain the drug and leave the pipe behind.

SMURFS Blue MDMA pills, the color of Smurf cartoon characters.

SNAPPERS Amyl or Butyl Nitrate SNAPS Street gang term for money.

SNIFF

a. To take cocaine, amphetamines or heroin by inhaling through the nose
b. To inhale solvents through both the nose and mouth

SNORT To inhale a drug in powdered form. Usually refers to Cocaine.

SNOT Black Tar Heroin.

SNOW Cocaine.

SNOW BIRD Cocaine.

SNOW FLAKE Cocaine.

SNOW BUGS The sensation of bugs crawling on or under the skin of a Cocaine user.

SNOW SEAL A brand of non-porous smooth paper used to make bindles to carry drugs. Logo is a seal balancing a snowflake on its nose.

SOAP GHB.

SOAPER/SOAP Sopor (Methaqualone).

SODIUM OXYBATE The drug GHB, tradename Xyrem.

SOFT DRUGS Drugs of abuse other than narcotics also applied to those drugs perceived to have low toxicity and/or dependency liability.

SOLES Slabs of solid Hashish.

SOMA Common street name and a tradename of the abused skeletal muscle relaxant carisoprodol, a depressant.

SOURCE A drug dealer or drug supplier.

SPACE BASING Freebased Cocaine dipped in PCP and then smoked.

SPACED Unresponsive to the external environment, usually in reaction to altered consciousness produced by hallucinogenic drugs.

SPACEY Referring to a strangeness or a state of psychic deterioration produced by excessive and/or heavy, chronic use of drugs.

SPEAKER TWEAKER People high on MDMA who hang onto the speakers at raves for the intense sensation of sound and vibration.

SPECIAL K The drug ketamine.

SPEED Injectable methamphetamine.

SPEEDBALL Heroin plus cocaine.

SPEEDFREAK Heavy regular use of injectable methamphetamine.

SPEED LAB Laboratory where Methamphetamines are manufactured.

SPEEDER Methamphetamine user.

SPICE Foil packets with names like Spice, Spice Gold, Spice Silver, Spice Diamond, Genie and Yucatan Fire "incense" test negative by standard marijuana testing, but have been laced with verifiable amounts of synthetic cannabinoids or cannabinoid-mimicking compounds, including HU-210, JWH-018 and other related chemicals. Also known as K2.

SPIKE Hypodermic needle.

SPOON

a. Small metal spoon used to snort (inhale) drugs in powdered form
b. Teaspoon used to heat drugs prior to injection
c. Street measurement of a drug, usually an amount for personal use and usually refers to Heroin

SPORE The reproductive part of the mushroom.

SPORTING Cocaine use.

STACKING The use of two or more steroids. One right after another, but not at the same time.

STAR DUST Cocaine.

STASH

a. A place where drugs are hidden to escape detection in the event of a sudden search by authorities
b. To hide drugs rapidly when confronted with a search

STASH CANS Common brand name items, such as beer cans, motor oil cans, in which the bottom or top screws off and the drugs are hidden inside.

STEP-ON To dilute a drug.

STICK A Marijuana cigarette.

STINK WEED Low grade Marijuana.

STONED Pleasurably intoxicated.

STOOLIE An informant.

S.T.P. Serenity, Tranquility, Peace. The synthetic hallucinogen 2,5-Dimethoxy-4-Methlyamphetamine.

STRAWBERRY Street gang term for a female who exchanges sex for drugs.

STRUNG OUT

a. In an emaciated and generally poor state of health and appearance due to chronic drug use
b. Heavily dependent on drugs
c. Sometimes to produce an extreme negative psychic effect during a single drug episode

STUFF General term for drugs, specifically Heroin.

SUGAR (MILK) HABIT Addict's desire for sweets due to heavy amount of milk mixed with everyday heroin.

SUNSHINE Long standing term for LSD but also a term for a new drug, methylmethcathinone, which is chemically similar to methcathinone (See methcathinone in stimulant section; see also MEPHEDRONE, MEOW MEOW).

SUPER GRASS

a. PCP laced Marijuana
b. High grade potent Marijuana

SUPER JOINT Marijuana cigarette dipped in PCP.

SUPER K The prescription drug Ketamine.

SUPER WEED

a. High grade Marijuana
b. Marijuana laced with PCP

SUPPLIER Drug dealer or drug source.

SWEAT IT OUT To withdraw from narcotic analgesics.

SWEEPING Snorting (inhaling) drugs in powdered form.

SWING MAN A drug supplier.

SWIRL or SWIRLING The drug GHB; the sensation of being on GHB

T The prescription drug Talwin.

T'S AND BLUES Pentazocine (Talwin) plus tripelennamine prepared in a solution and injected.

TABS LSD.

TAKE-OFF The first effects of a drug.

TAR Mexican black tar heroin.

TASTE Sampling a drug before buying it.

TATTOOING Prior to injecting, some users burn the end of the needle for sterilization. If the carbon deposits that form are not cleaned off prior to injecting, they will form under the skin causing dark marks. Same principle as a standard tattoo.

TEA Marijuana.

TEABAGGING Rectal insertion of tampon soaked in GHB.

TEMPLE BALLS Hashish mixed with Opium then shaped into a small, round ball. Common in Nepal and parts of India.

TEN CENTS Ten dollars.

TEN CENT BAG Ten dollars worth of a drug.

TETRAHYDROZOLINE The active ingredient in Visine© and other eye drop brands; has been used to incapacitate people for purposes of robbery and as a dangerous prank; ingestion can result in blurred vision, lowering of blood pressure, seizures, coma; abusers of GHB and drug rapists often utilize eye drop bottles to hide and transport GHB.

TFMPP The drug TFMPP or 1-(3-Trifluoromethylphenyl) piperazine is referred to as Molly and is typically in capsule form; same clientele as MDMA and similar effects (See MOLLY and BZP).

THAI STICK Potent Marijuana from Thailand whose buds are attached to six inch sticks with string.

THC Delta 9-Tetrahydrocannabinol. The active ingredient of the Marijuana plant.

THE MATRIX The cough suppressant DXM, referring to the red pill of Coricidin® Cough & Cold and the movie by that name wherein a red pill is taken to enter the matrix.

THRUSTERS Amphetamines.

TIE A tourniquet tied around the arm to inhibit blood flow so the vein will bulge for injecting. Example: Belt, scarf, hose, surgical tubing, etc.

TIE UP To apply a belt or tourniquet to the arm or leg to produce distention of a vein for an injection.

TIE RAG (See TIE).

TIME FLIP The flip of MDMA and DMT (See FLIP and DMT).

TMA Trimethoxyamphetamine. Similar to MDA.

TOKE
a. A puff of a marijuana cigarette
b. To take a puff

TOKER Marijuana smoker.

TOOLS Drug paraphernalia.

TOOT Cocaine.

TOOTER A piece of a drinking straw, a rolled up dollar bill, or other device used for snorting (inhaling) powdered drugs.

TOPS The top buds of the Marijuana plant rich in THC.

TOTALED Exhausted after an acute drug experience.

TRACKS, TRACK MARKS
a. Collapsed veins resulting from chronic injection
b. discoloration and scars, resembling a tattoo in appearance, resulting from chronic injection

TRAIL MIX Abuse of multiple prescription drugs and/or over the counter products (See PHARMING).

TRANK PCP.

TRAVELER A user of hallucinogenic drugs.

TREATMENT A dose of Heroin, especially when feeling the effects of withdrawal.

TRIP Under the influence of a drug. Usually refers to LSD.

TRIPPERS LSD.

TRIPLE C Dextromethorphan (See CCC and DXM).

TRIPLE STACK An Ecstasy pill three times the normal thickness and dosage.

TRYPTAMINES Class of chemical compounds that produce hallucinogenic effects, most notorious being psilocybin mushrooms, DMT, 2C-T-7, AMT and FOXY.

TUIES The prescription drug Tuinal.

TURN ON
a. To produce a state of pleasurable excitement (the stimulus may be either a drug or other experience)
b. To introduce someone to a drug or drugs

TWEAKED Under the influence of Methamphetamine sometimes refers to an adverse reaction.

TWEAKER Chronic meth abuser at the end of a binge period. This is a dangerous time for confrontation with law enforcement due to high propensity for violence at this stage.

UNCUT A drug that has not been diluted.

UP FRONT
a. As a sample, a small quantity of a drug is provided to the buyer to indicate quality
b. As proof, showing the seller the money before the drugs are produced

UPPERS A general term used for most stimulant drugs of abuse, such as amphetamines, and related drugs. However, the term is not used for cocaine.

UP TIGHT Tense, nervous or frightened because of a subjective experience produced by either a drug or by real events.

URINE METH Saving urine from chronic users to process for the unmetabolized meth.

USER Someone who uses drugs or is an addict.

U.S.P. Pharmaceutical Methamphetamine.

VALS The prescription drug Valium.

VAPORS Gang term for Freebase Cocaine smoke.

VEGETABLE One who suffers from severe brain or behavioral impairment to the point of being unable to care for oneself.

VITAMIN K The drug ketamine (See SPECIAL K).

WACK
a. To dilute or cut a drug
b. PCP

WAFER COCAINE Rock cocaine in appearance of wafers or pasta style (instead of the typical "rock" format), classic of 18th Street Gang.

WAKE-UPS Amphetamines.

WASHBACK A method used to get any usable drug out of a pipe after it has been used several times (See WASHBACK METHODS).

WASTED Exhausted after an acute drug experience, usually in reference to amphetamines or cocaine.

WATER
a. Methamphetamine
b. GHB

WATER PIPE A smoking pipe that has a chamber that is filled with water or wine. The chamber is used to cool the smoke (See BONG).

WEDGES Flat LSD tablets.

WEED
a. Marijuana
b. Tobacco

WEEKENDER An occasional drug user.

WET DADDIES PCP.

WETS Marijuana cigarettes dipped in PCP and/or embalming fluid (See FRYS, PCP, EMBALMING FLUID, ILLY).

WHIP-ITS or WHIPPITS or WHIPPETS Small nitrous oxide canisters, slightly smaller than CO2 cartridges, used to power whipped cream makers and often abused by inhalation (See CRACKERS, NITROUS OXIDE, N2O).

WHITE
a. Cocaine
b. Asian Heroin

WHITE GIRL Cocaine.

WHITES Amphetamine tablets.

WHITE STUFF Heroin, usually Chinese.

WIGGIN or WIGGING
a. Bizarre behavior on mind-altering drugs
b. in need of drugs
c. on MDMA (Ecstasy)

WINDOW PANE LSD that is placed on small squares of gelatin.

WIPED OUT To have lost consciousness from abusing drugs.

WIRED
a. Chronically dependent on amphetamines
b. Physically dependent on heroin

WIRED-OUT High on Cocaine or Methamphetamine.

WITHDRAW The effects of quitting the heavy use of narcotics.

WORKS Paraphernalia for injecting drugs.

WRECKED
a. Exhausted after an acute drug experience
b. Having a very bad drug experience

X MDMA (3,4-Methylenedioxly-N-Mtheylamphetamine).

XTC Also known as Ecstacy, MDMA, and Adam. Psychedelic drug common to "rave" parties.

YABA Also called the CRAZY DRUG, YABA is simply pills of meth or a combo of meth/ephedrine; designed to market to teens with the pill format, colors and logos, similar to MDMA marketing.

YELLOWS or YELLOW JACKETS Nembutal (Pentobarbital sodium).

YEN Agitated sleep occurring during withdrawal from heroin.

Z One ounce of a drug.

ZANY BARS The drug alprazolam, tradename Xanax, a benzodiazepine depressant; refers to the format sometimes used for this drug which is bars with marks for breaking off doses as directed.

ZIP/ZIPPY Amphetamines.

ZOMBIE DRUG See SCOPOLAMINE.

ZONKED Extremely high on drugs.

D

E

F

Q

R

S